Social Entrepreneurship as Sustainable Development

Tamara L. Stenn

Social Entrepreneurship as Sustainable Development

Introducing the Sustainability Lens

palgrave
macmillan

Tamara L. Stenn
SIT Graduate Institute
Brattleboro, Vermont, USA

ISBN 978-3-319-48059-6 ISBN 978-3-319-48060-2 (eBook)
DOI 10.1007/978-3-319-48060-2

Library of Congress Control Number: 2016956868

Printed on acid-free paper

This Palgrave Macmillan imprint is published by Springer Nature
The registered company is Springer International Publishing AG
The registered company address is: Gewerbestrasse 11, 6330 Cham, Switzerland

I dedicate this book to the memory of my father and entrepreneur,
Richard S. Stenn

Preface

This is a book about how anyone can become a social entrepreneur and engage in sustainable development. It introduces the sustainability lens (SL), a practical tool I spent 18 years developing, and shows how it brings into focus the necessary considerations and actions needed to build a more just and sustainable world. I encourage readers to use the lens to build sustainability in their own lives and organizations. This tool is presented for use in the classroom and with businesses worldwide. It functions with high-school students, college students, graduates, start-ups, microenterprises, nonprofit and for-profit organizations, corporations, communities, and teams. We are all entrepreneurs in how we make choices in our production and consumption and through these actions we each have the power to affect change as we wish and build a more just and sustainable world. This book will show you how.

Sustainability can be defined as a long-term balance that is not harmful to others or depletes resources. When paired with development, sustainability becomes a construction maintained over time that does not damage the environment and protects the interests of current and future generations. Overall, sustainable development is an intentional, closed-loop model where inputs and outputs are balanced and materials are transformed and reused in self-perpetuating ways. Sustainability can be understood in the natural world when complex, symbiotic relationships from around the transformation of matter for the benefit and development of all.

For example, an apple tree makes energy through the development of leaves and photosynthesis, creating flowers that bees pollinate and from which fruit forms. The fruit feeds other animals and bears seeds that propagate the species. The leaves are shed in the fall and become compost which later feeds the tree and communities around it. In addition, flowers provide nectar for butterflies and pollen for bees who use it to make honey. Collectively many different entities benefit from and are dependent upon the tree for their well-being forming either direct or indirect relationships with the tree and each other.

The tree is also dependent upon these often transient or indirect relationships for its own well-being. For example, the tree needs the bee as a pollinator and the bee needs pollen. However, any bee can pollinate any flower and the same bee may never visit the same tree again. For the moment, though, they are supporting each other and that is important. These relationships either fleeting, like that of the bee, or more long term such as that of the colonies of fungi which live among tree roots breaking down debris into minerals that can be absorbed by the tree are essential for the survival of all. Looking at sustainable development from a nature-based perspective creates a systems way of thinking where complex and simple relationships become visible, and new complexities and creativity transform resources in needed ways.

Taking a nature-based view on development is not new. For thousands of years, indigenous people worldwide have used nature systems to shape their way of organizing societies and making decisions. For example, the idea of seven generations was a common measurement native people in the United States used to determine if a new approach was worth pursuing. They imagined the impact of choices made from a perspective of 175 years in the future, if the impact seemed positive then the approach would be adopted, if not, it would be abandoned (Vecsey and Venables 1994). This sentiment is echoed in Native American Chief Oren Lyons of the Onondaga Nation's writing, "We are looking ahead, as is one of the first mandates given us as chiefs, to make sure and to make every decision that we make relate to the welfare and well-being of the seventh generation to come . . . What about the seventh generation? Where are you taking them? What will they have?" (Vecsey and Venables 1994, pp. 173–174). In today's fast-paced word, it is difficult to even consider the next generation in decision making, little let alone the seventh. However, slowing down and taking the time to think about the long view is key in understanding and building sustainable development.

This book introduces models I have studied, taught, and lived for many years which are relevant to our understanding of sustainable development today. One is the science of permaculture (permanent agriculture) which, developed in the 1970s, uses nature systems to work with forces such as wind, sun, water, and landscapes to provide food, shelter, and other needs with minimum labor while nourishing the earth. Another is social solidarity economy which since the 1980s has focused on creatively getting needs met collectively through production and distribution using diverse economic approaches such as barter, trade, and worker cooperatives. I also bring in the Andean model of Suma Qamana, which based on pre-Inca indigenous wisdom introduces ancient ways used today to work together and celebrate our shared humanity. And I introduce the model of Circles of Sustainability, a collectively developed method of measurement created in the 1990s which quantifies and defines sustainability in place-based environments. Together, these form the SL which is presented here as a tool to grow social enterprises and build our own sustainable development. The reason why I begin with enterprises is because they are the accessible, have tremendous power, and, as an entrepreneur myself, I know them well.

This book is about social entrepreneurship (SE) as sustainable development but it actually begins with any type of entrepreneurship. As ideas are discovered and implemented through the use of the SL, organizations naturally move toward a state of SE. It is these social entrepreneurs who move toward sustainable development and anyone with the right mind-set can be a social entrepreneur.

J. Greg Dees, the father of SE, defines it as a change-based process that creates social value through bold innovation and creativity (Dees 1998). SE functions alongside non-SE enterprises and is largely understood as a business development option. However, SE is not merely a business development option, rather it is a key component of sustainable development. Recognizing SE as a way of being, rather than a business model, highlights ways which all are engaged in SE through daily interactions and choices as consumers, workers, and creators, thus building an important link between SE and sustainability and giving everyone a role in participating in.

However, social enterprises are not necessarily sustainable. Some may be missing mechanisms and guidelines for growth, management, energy use, regeneration, or community building. Sustainability is about bringing balance and equilibrium to growth and ensuring a viable future. An SE is a good place to start for building sustainability because many of the values and intent needed for sustainability exist in the social enterprise model; however, moving from social to sustainable is both a small and large a step. This is because of the interconnectedness and vastness of sustainability. In a small step, the SL presented here can help a single social enterprise become more sustainable in its own right simply through informed, educated decisions and practices. Nevertheless, this enterprise can still be left vulnerable and unsustainable by nonaligned enterprises.

As resources become scarce and technology brings the world closer together, it is becoming increasingly evident that unless we all work together in a unified system of sustainability, the human race will be in grave danger. As Eric Cooperström of the Skoll Foundation wrote after the 2015 UN Climate Change Conference, COP21, "We're in this together as a global community, and everyone—from governments, to business, to civil society and beyond—must do their part to ensure a sustainable future."

One cannot build sustainability alone. Like concentric circles, livelihoods and interactions overlap. A nonpolluting, thoughtfully functioning, right-sized, sustainable social enterprise is still impacted by the same acid rain, climate change, and contamination as the rest of the world, no matter how green they may personally be. This is the big step. However, a big step is formed by many small ones. The more the SL is shared and used, the more aligned enterprises can become in their sustainability and the smaller that "big step" becomes. Until now, there has not been a comprehensive, systematic approach toward building sustainability. The SL changes this.

Chapter 1 goes deeper into the question of "why sustainability?" It introduces key terms and examines the idea of sustainability from the perspective of a shared global environment where the actions of one affect all. Here the ideas of Suma Qamana and Circles of Sustainability, which form the base of the SL, are more deeply explored.

Chapter 2 explains in detail with case study examples, what each other the four quadrants of the SL are, and how they can be understood and realized in today's business environment. The four SL quadrants are resources—where things come from; health—impact and engagement; policy—advocacy and influence; and exchange—accessibility and distribution.

Chapter 3 brings new ideas based on economic permaculture and social solidarity economy, to illuminate, inspire, and create practical, innovative approaches in response to needs and challenges identified through the SL.

Chapter 4 introduces the Business Model Canvas (BMC) which is an open-source, design-thinking tool that revolutionizes the way businesses are imagined and communicated. In step-by-step detail, each of the four quadrants of the SL is applied to the nine sections of the BMC, creating an array of 36 different angles and approaches for imagining and realizing sustainable development. The nine sections are key partners, key activities, key resources, value proposition, customer relationships, channels, customer segments, cost structure, and revenue streams. Together these form a complete business map.

Chapter 5 takes a step back to look at the SL's SE as sustainable development from the perspective of Amartya Sen's *Ideas of Justice* and the capabilities approach.

Acknowledgments

I would like to thank my father the late Richard Stenn for his inspiration as an entrepreneur. This book would also not have been possible if it were not for my amazing, inquisitive, inspiring students at Hampshire College and Mount Holyoke College and my entrepreneurship colleagues at the Grinspoon Foundation especially Cari Carpenter, Elizabeth Long Lingo, and Thom Simmons; UMass colleague Bogdan Prokopovych; and Paul Silva and the Valley Venture Mentor enthusiasts. Thank you for the opportunity to share practices, ideas, and resources on entrepreneurship and support the growth of student entrepreneurs. Also big thanks to collaborator and colleague Hendrik Van den Berg and his thoughtful conversations which encouraged the development of this book; to Jim Verzino for supporting the graphical development of the sustainability lens; to Emily Kawano for her thoughtful conversations about solidarity economy; and to Sarango for his insights and deep work on Suma Qamana. I also want to recognize the work of Liam Magee, Paul James, and Andy Scerri in supporting and guiding me in the use and development of the Circles of Sustainability model in my Fulbright research.

Contents

Abbreviations

BMC	Business Model Canvas
CSU	Colorado State University
CC	Creative Commons
DOE	Department of Energy
IK	Indigenous knowledge
LDC	Least developed countries
NCA	National Confectioners Association
PLM	Product life cycle management
SE	Social entrepreneurship
SRI	Socially responsible investing
SSE	Social solidarity economy
SL	Sustainability lens
UNDP	United Nations Development Program

List of Figures

List of Tables

CHAPTER 1

Building the Lens

Abstract This chapter goes deeper into the question of "why sustainability?" It introduces key terms and examines the idea of sustainability from the perspective of a shared global environment where the actions of one affect all. Here the ideas of Suma Qamana and Circles of Sustainability, which form the base of the sustainability lens, are more deeply explored.

Keywords Circles of Sustainability · United Nations Development Programs (UNDP) · Globalization · Business Model Canvas · Suma Qamana · Transparency · Economics

Why Sustainability?

We live in a globalized world. Globalization can be defined as a "process of extension and intensification of social relations across world-space, where the nature of world-space is understood in terms of the temporal frame or of the social imaginary in which that space is lived—ecologically, economically, politically and culturally" (Circles of Sustainability, p. 28). This means that one is socially connected on many levels through nature, trade, politics, and culture. A social connection is one that relates to society and community and is focused on collective group participation as opposed to individuality. Though one may identify strongly as an individual, they are in fact dependent on being a part of a collective whole and dependent on each other for survival. Our globalization is a

T.L. Stenn, *Social Entrepreneurship as Sustainable Development*,
DOI 10.1007/978-3-319-48060-2_1

vulnerability, and also a strength. As we realize our global vulnerability, we can also realize opportunities to reduce risks and grow more sustainability.

A wise Andean scholar once told me that one can be the most perfect, beautiful leaf, but without the tree, they are just compost. A leaf is a leaf because it is a part of a tree. The tree is the collective whole that supports the individual, whether identified as so or not. It is in this collective dependency that vulnerability exists and sustainability becomes important.

As previously noted, sustainability is a long-term balance that is not harmful to others nor depletes resources while it also protects the interests of current and future generations. The vulnerability here is the loss of balance. If one is overusing resources or engaging in harmful practices such as human rights abuses or environmental contamination, then the balance is lost. This loss of balance is often not directly experienced or seen by the perpetrator. An example of this is found in the effects of climate change brought about by the well-documented continual increase in atmospheric greenhouse gas concentrations produced by industrialized nations and a 160-year record of direct temperature measurements (Thompson 2010). This phenomenon is causing a dramatic rise in global temperatures and the loss of delicate tropical glaciers in the Andes, Himalayas, and on Mount Kilimanjaro (Thompson 2010). These glaciers, largely located in least developed countries (LDCs)—which have very low greenhouse gas emissions—support fragile ecosystems and supply water to faraway aquifers. With the glaciers gone, the aquifers dry up leaving individuals in cities and on farms many miles away struggling to find water to sustain themselves. Though the LDCs and the aquifer-dependent communities may have been careful in their use of resources—being a healthy leaf in the analogy of the tree—they suffer from the consequence of the actions of others. The tree itself is sick and this affects the "healthy" leaf too. A leaf cannot leave one tree and go to another. It must wait and hope things get better, or break off and fall to the ground, turning to compost and no longer being a leaf. In this case, the tree is our planet and as leaves, if one can no longer be sustained then one, like the leaf, has no option but to fall onto the earth and turn into compost too. Researcher and paleoclimatologist, Lonnie Thompson, noted that in the case of the global glaciers there are three options: "mitigation, adaptation, and suffering" (2010, p. 153). A fourth option is also death. The sustainability lens (SL) addresses mitigation, creating new ways in which to imagine and use resources, share knowledge, and build community to affect positive change.

If we wait for governments, it'll be too late.
If we act as individuals, it'll be too little.
But if we act as communities, it might just be enough, just in time.

(Rob Hopkins, founder of the Transition movement commenting on [2011, p. 17])

Rob Hopkins is a permaculture professor and founder of Transition, a global social movement focused on growing sustainability in a post-peak oil environment. He noted in his quote that government lacks the agility needed to grow sustainability and individuals simply do not have the power to make real change on their own; however, communities do have both power and agility.

Taking the idea of community to "business" creates a new dynamic where resources and market forces drive change moving from beyond a community-based volunteer model to that of a viable business with a competitive incentive and access to resources. This is why the SL is being presented as a tool to work with businesses. Businesses, through their collective actions to create saleable products and services, have tremendous power to affect positive change. They can influence sustainability through supply chain management, employee relations, and community involvement. In addition, businesses through the products and services they provide can set the example, educate others, and advocate for changes to grow sustainably. Businesses have influence over vendors and contractors with their buying power; influence over workers with their policies and procedures; influence over community by their actions; and influence over consumers by their messages and goods delivered. In this way, businesses are the powerhouse saviors that can lead the way to regain balance and growing sustainability in our world today and a viable future for generations to come tomorrow.

To change paths, take a leadership role, and embrace sustainability is a tall order for a business that is working hard enough just to keep their current profit-driven model functioning. Often businesses ask why sustainability is even important, why they should engage in it, and if it really matters. Many companies feel they are doing good enough, they understand their environment, markets, customers, strengths, and weaknesses well and see no need to change how they operate or even consider looking at things differently. They are functioning, comfortable, and busy with more immediate daily challenges and operations. Unfortunately, continuing to contribute to the imbalance of the planet today will have dire consequences tomorrow.

Rose Marcario, CEO of Patagonia, a company deeply committed to sustainable development, reflected upon this, looking back at her own transition from being a powerful leader in profit-driven enterprises to her current work as CEO Patagonia. At Patagonia, values come before profit but do not replace it. Marcario helped Patagonia to double its scale of operations and triple its profits, with about $600 million in revenues in 2013, while still actively building sustainability (Baer 2014).

"That (value driven lens) is a very different lens than the corporate-public world where I grew up in, where most decisions were made solely for the profit of the financial shareholders. I had lived and worked in that world before I came to Patagonia, and I can tell you that is the road to hell—we will destroy the planet with that mindset" (Baer 2014).

Sustainability does not just happen. It needs to be sought out, pursued, embraced, and shared. It takes time, energy, commitment, and tenacity but it works. The beauty of the SL is that it can be used thoroughly or lightly as one wants. Think of it as a magnifying lens. Depending on how it is held—from further away things are amplified in a more general way, and by holding the lens up close, smaller things become visible and very tiny details can be carefully examined. It is up to the user how they want to hold and focus the lens.

The Business Model Canvas (BMC) is a perfect map over which to run the SL. Created as a design-thinking tool for building conversation around business strategy and development, it encompasses all aspects of growing and managing a business (Strategyzer.com 2016). Adding a sustainability focus to this gives owners the tools and knowledge to choose to become a more sustainable enterprise. How the lens is used is up the business itself. Using the SL to do a brief overview of the business map can bring some quick ideas into focus and even highlight previously unseen risks, vulnerabilities, or easy opportunities. The lens can be used to create a general "to list" and timeline, identifying places where more work can be done at later dates. It can also be used to identify where committees or projects can be developed to support the deeper scrutiny of a particular area.

The SL is about finding opportunity, seeing areas of positive change, and improving well-being for all, the business, workers, local community, and environment. It works with the assumption that people are good and everyone wants to leave the earth a better place for their offspring and future generations while also enjoying a level of success and feeling of well-being and accomplishment in their own lives. The SL is designed to be used in that way, to bring into focus win–win situations that elevate the well-being of all: the practitioner, community, and customers. It is not meant to be imposing or punishing, rather it is meant to be illuminating and enlightening identifying areas of positive growth, impact, and meaning.

The fact is that without sustainability, we all are vulnerable. Though a company may feel healthy and well positioned now, as humans together on a finite planet, we all put each other at risk by not thinking more sustainability about our collective futures. Right now we are at a place of luxury where much of our work toward sustainability is proactive and preventative; being done as mitigation. We are not in survival mode yet, but in time this will shift as resources continue to become more scarce and change less predictable. The SL is presented here as tool to influence the long-term impact that we can have in making the world a better, more balanced, sustainable place for all and avoid having to enter into a struggle for survival.

Suma Qamana—A Personal Story

While studying sustainability as a graduate student, I found myself asking, "How did it used to get done? What were the systems used for thousands of years that got us to where we are today? What systems have been lost or forgotten? And when was a time when we all lived in more balanced harmony with the world around us?" I began looking for examples of longevity and the systems that supported it. It was 2007. In the Andean region where I worked, as a Peace Corps volunteer, social entrepreneur, and researcher, others were beginning to ask the same thing. When Bolivian indigenous leader, Evo Morales, was elected president in 2009, more attention and value was given to the work of indigenous scholars across the Andean regions. The Andean region is made up of the countries of Ecuador, Colombia, Peru, and Bolivia.

Suma Qamana (soo'mah—ka'ma-na) means "living well" in the Andean language of Quechua. This is presented as an alternative to the western idea of "living better"—than everyone else. Suma Qamana is also known as Sumaq(k) Kasway in Aymara and Vivir Bien in Spanish. It is a holistic Andean model of grassroots sustainable development, governance, and policy (Choquehuanca 2010). Ecuadorian economist Pablo Davalos proclaims that within the discussion of economic policy, "the one that presents more options within its theoretical and epistemological framework to replace the old notions of development and economic growth is Sumak Kawsay, good living" (Thomson 2011, p. 452).

Suma Qamana is based on the four quadrants or directions of the Chakana or Andean Cross, a constellation seen only in the Southern Hemispheres, and functions in harmony and equilibrium with people and nature. The Chakana depicts the ideological and mythical basis of Suma Qamana sustainable development. The challenges of each learning center are present in each of its four points. These challenges are to rebuild the world vision and transcend national and regional barriers; recover the idea of a living world; relearn human life skills; and impart the urgency of having a cross-cultural perspective and an ongoing quest for wisdom (Garcia et al. 2004, p. 309).

Suma Qamana is a proposal born in the community and is based not on the logic of economic profitability, but on producing goods according to nature, and meeting needs with limits and careful use of resources (Garcia et al. 2004). Suma Qamana gained much international attention when it was endorsed by the United Nations in 2009 as a viable approach to sustainability and adopted into new constitutions written by each of the Andean nations: Bolivia, Ecuador, Colombia, and Peru (Monni and Pallottino 2013).

"We don't believe in the linear, cumulative conception of progress and of an unlimited development at the cost of other people and of nature," explained President Morales, "to live well is to think not only in terms of per capita income, but of cultural identity, community, harmony among ourselves and with Mother Earth" (Hernandez Navarro 2012).

Andean scholars share a cultural belief in Pachakuti, literally "earth movement" in Quechua, a foretold turning or reversal of the world (Aguilar and Skar 2014). They feel we are now in Pachakuti, a time of great change, and feel a collective mandate to bring indigenous knowledge (IK) beyond their borders to share with global society. In the early 2000s, indigenous scholars in Ecuador and surrounding Andean nations came together and with the help of United Nations Educational Cultural and Scientific Organization (UNESCO) formed Amawtay Wasi (House of Knowledge in Quechua), the world's first accredited indigenous university, with learning based on indigenous epistemology (Sarango 2009). This indigenous epistemology, like many IK systems, is holistic, adaptable, dynamic, and presented in an experiential learning pedagogy (Battiste 2002). Learning takes place in four stages, related to the four points of the Chakana: theories are established, applied, experienced, and then observed and reflected upon.

I was intrigued. I found the work of Amawtay Wasi and the multicultural, interdisciplinary nature of IK to be very relevant in the business world. Over time I met with indigenous scholars and followed their work, thinking how it related to my own experiences and observations as a business person and global citizen outside of the Andean region. The ideas and belief systems of Amawtay Wasi influenced how I understood Suma Qamana, giving me a deeper understanding of its meaning and context.

By 2007, I was ready to begin building Suma Qamana into my own business, KUSIKUY, a US-based Fair Trade fashion company that supplies Bolivian-made, handknit alpaca clothing to markets worldwide. I examined KUSIKUY from Suma Qamana's different quadrants and found it very useful for identifying new programs to launch, imagine more inclusive ways to fund the company, and discover better ways to build interactions with clients and producers. I enjoyed the creativity and inclusiveness Suma Qamana brought to our business and felt it would be helpful to share with others.

However, Suma Qamana was an Andean model. It worked well with my company, which had production in the Andean region, a place with strong community and a highly collective culture, key components of Suma Qamana philosophy. But would it work in a highly individualistic culture such as the United States? To find out, over the course of 5 years, I presented and published several articles and papers about Suma Qamana as a sustainable development tool and created a series of participant-based workshops and university curricula to explore Suma Qamana in entrepreneurship and community development—grounding it in economic and political science disciplines. What emerged was a more open inclusive, flexible, practical, and creative way of approaching sustainability, both culturally and economically.

I discovered Suma Qamana worked across cultures, languages, and socioeconomic divides. It highlighted the collective universality of our human roots and was easily understood and engaged in. As humans, we all share the same desires for well-being, personal fulfillment, supportive community, and meaningful work. Rooted in ancient, indigenous traditions, Suma Qamana transcended individual country, language, and culture differences. It placed us at a collective one, a mixed people of the same race, and a single humanity and was uniquely unifying in that way.

For example to live well, writes David Choquehuanca, Bolivia's Foreign Minister, one must know how to, "nourish themselves, drink, dance, sleep, work, meditate, love and be loved, listen, hear, be able to express themselves, and walk" (Choquehuanca 2010, p. 3).

Suma Qamana is an essential element of the SL. It transforms the lens from being an endless "to do" checklist to something more personal, relatable, fun, and engaging. It brings a human element to the task of building sustainability and helps to create feelings of camaraderie through its focus on community and inclusiveness.

Defining Suma Qamana

Looking at Suma Qamana from the perspective of the four points of the Chakana creates a dynamic, holistic way in understanding sustainability. These points are Yahcay—knowing, Munay—loving, Ruray—doing, and Ushay—power. The center is Kausay—wisdom. The names come from the Quechua language and, in the Andean region, inform everyday decision making and policy. When looking at these four points through a business lens, they bring into focus items needed for building business sustainability. The following is a more detailed interpretation of how these points can be realized in a business environment.

Yachay

Yachay, knowing, is about being aware of the world around you and how it interrelates. It is also about developing expertise, building skills, acquiring knowledge, and embracing diversity especially in others' worldviews and rationalities (Garcia et al. 2004). I think of Yachay as a resource area. I find when using Yachay in my business, I am taking more time to learn where things come from, how materials are made and sourced, where my energy use is coming from, and what the environmental impact of my actions are.

A common theme in Suma Qamana and Andean philosophy is that of opposites. Opposites, it is believed, form a whole (Huanacuni Mamani 2010). So, for example, having a narrow economic perspective with a focus on local trade and protective policies or a broad economic perspective that embraces global trade and trade agreements is not viewed as conflictive, rather it believed that together they form part of a complete way of economic being. Both are held together and are equally valued with no on being right, wrong, or better than the other. This is often hard to grasp in the more linear and judgmental way people view business, but it also opens one to more possibilities. One must remember that opposites make a whole and intentionally seek that opposite for balance. This creates a different feeling of possibility, erases feelings of "otherness," competition or disdain, and results in stronger, further reaching solutions.

Because Yachay has diversity (and the embracing of opposites) as a core value, I find myself being less judgmental when I encounter unsustainable business practices. For example, the large carbon footprint of the air travel my handmade products go through at KUSIKUY as they move from Bolivia to the United States and to customers worldwide contrasts sharply with our policy of engaging in hand labor and zero fossil fuel use in production. Embracing Yachay in the full Andean sense of opposites creating a whole enables us to recognize this dynamic and work toward solving it, rather than try to hide or ignore it.

Munay

Munay refers to loving and the need to be passionate about something. It encompasses emotions, intuition, transcendence, affection, willpower, consent, affection, self-esteem, friendship, mysticism, and the ability to think with the heart (Garcia et al. 2004). In traditional business models, this can often be looked as "soft skills" and left to the Human Resource Department to develop. However, Suma Qamana is a total way of being and a model that is both wholly embraced individually and organizationally (Huanacuni Mamani 2010). In the workplace, I have found Munay to be associated with volunteerism and celebration; some people call this "morale." Businesses that have strong Munay always seem to do better than those who do not. They see to have lower turnover, higher productivity, and more fun. Munay is the one area that seems the most deficient in many western organizations but is part of the glue that holds the entire structure together. Without the soul, energy, and hearts of the members of the organization, there is no spirit to keep the organization alive.

I think of Munay as a health area. I find when using Munay in my business, I am taking more care to make sure people have work they are passionate about, they feel valued and well compensated for their work. I also make sure we take time to celebrate even small successes and have a positive, supportive environment where mistakes are laughed at, risk is encouraged—for example to try something new—shared and collectively solved.

Ruray

Ruray refers to action and doing. It is the capacity to produce, build, generate, implement, experiment, develop, and innovate both on a product or service level and on a personal level (Garcia et al. 2004). This aspect of self-development and the vulnerability it implies is particularly important. So is the idea of experiment, because this implies that the outcomes are unknown. With the Andean embracing of opposites, as seen in Yachay (knowing), Ruray can be achieved when there is both failure and success, as both are opposite sides of the whole process and are embraced as necessary parts. By being able to take the risk to imagine and act on something new or different opens the way for more creativity in the workforce as it gives permission for new ideas to be tried, and not always work out!

I think of Ruray as a creative policy area. I find when using Ruray in my business, I am taking time to develop systems that work together, engaging others in exploring new ways of doing things, forming alliances and collaboration across different departments, and moving away from traditional workflow models. For example, in the spirit of Ruray we work collaboratively with customers, knitters, and designers when creating new products; without Ruray, we would have left the work solely to the designer.

Ushay

Ushay is power, force, energy, vitality, and also the potential and possibility for this. It is power over one's environment and over others as well, for example, in decision-making and authoritative capacities (Garcia et al. 2004). However, Ushay is cross-cultural, as is all of Suma Qamana. This means that power is not just simply exerted, but is also reflected upon. This is very important. The cross-cultural aspect of Ushay leads to not just action, but also reflection on the results of that action. Dialogue and debate are essential elements of Ushay and again opposites are often embraced.

For example in my business, before Suma Qamana, we worked hard to generate as many orders as possible, offering high-quality product at affordable pricing with our earnings coming from the volume of goods produced. The push was to make more and more. However, the dynamic of too much Ushay (force or energy) caused people to get burnt out and stressed from so much work. They were out of balance; however, no one wanted to stop because they wanted the money. It was a vicious cycle that was wearing the people down.

In Suma Qamana we learned that Ushay was not just doing but also reflection. Through reflection, we thought about where we were, what was happening, and what we needed and wanted. We realized that if we changed our model and charged more for our work, we would have less demand for product and less work, but higher per piece earnings. With the higher earnings, we argued, we would still be able to make ends meet. It was a leap of faith. It seemed counterintuitive to purposely slow down sales by raising prices and making our product less accessible, but we did it and it worked. Later in the spirit of social solidarity economy, addressed later in this book, we developed ways to make the higher priced products more accessible to people who could not afford the pricing through trade, bulk buying, barter, and recycling—making used products available for people.

I often think of Ushay as the motor that drives the Suma Qamana circle and keeps it spinning, engaging the other quadrants and moving everything forward. When using Ushay in my business, it is the moment of gumption, the extra push I give myself or others when it is time to jump in and just do it. Though I also think of it as the “check engine light” that when creating space for reflection and evaluation, new possibilities can be seen. Ushay creates action and inadvertently leads to change.

Kawsay

Suma Qamana is unique in that it also has a center, that of Kawsay wisdom. Kawsay has to do with life and the spiral aspect of it. Unlike western models, Andean time is dimensional and understood as a huge moving spiral. This means that the future is forever moving into the present which is simultaneously passing into the past (Garcia et al. 2004). Our singular moments of being are part of a much greater lineage that extends thousands of years down to our ancestors and thousands of years up to future generations. There is no beginning or end, rather we are part of it all now together. The present becomes the past as the future moves into the present. This worldview creates a feeling of solidarity and togetherness in the moment and a deep connection to a shared past and future. Kasway in the Suma Qamana tradition is manifested in living well with simplicity, humility, harmony, transparency, inspiration, silence, and a deep knowledge that individually we know nothing but instead are a part of a much larger whole (Garcia et al. 2004). This leads to feelings of freedom as one lets go through still is held by the collective spiral. As Amawtay Wasi, the world's first accredited indigenous University located in Ecuador explains, Kasway is "a sailing adrift in a deep state of alertness, letting life live, and walking without a path" (Garcia et al. 2004, p. 310). This is a big leap of faith, but when achieved, the feeling is amazing.

I often feel Kasway with my business when I am engaging in social media and sending pixels out to the universe, to an imagined audience. When likes come back and followers are found, I feel that universal spiral encompassing us and know we are on the right track, being pulled together by our collective understanding of art, style, and values, moving along life's spiral together.

Circles of Sustainability

At the same time that I was exploring and implementing Suma Qamana sustainability, the United Nations was also exploring and defining sustainable development goals. Conferences, meetings, and working groups were formed with scholars and practitioners from around the globe coming together to share models, ideas, and experiences. A conversation at a United Nations Development Program (UNDP) conference led to the creation of an interdisciplinary, international task force to study sustainability in urban environments (circlesofsustainability.org 2014). From 2012 to 2014, scores of scholars and developers from Germany, Australia, Canada, and the United States worked together, exploring different ways in which to define and measure sustainability (circlesofsustainability.org 2014). Work was informed from conferences, presentations, pilot studies, and case studies from New Guinea, Brazil, India, Malta, Spain, China, UAE, and more (circlesofsustainability.org 2014). Over time, patterns began to emerge and a common language developed. This became known as the Circle project and focused on the continued formation and exploration of what eventually became known as the Circles of Sustainability.

In the Circles project, sustainable development is understood as improving social resilience, security, and adaptability through local development (James 2015). It is a participant-based appraisal model where stakeholders are asked what sustainability means to them, how it is achieved for them, what resources are needed for them to support this, and how they would want these resources acquired and used without compromising the ability of future generations' ability to meet their own needs (James 2015).

Stakeholders are anyone who is affected by living in, or the actions of, a particular region. Needs are understood more broadly, going beyond economics to include cultural, political, and ecological concerns. Since needs are dynamic and constantly evolving, studying sustainable development becomes a highly participatory, dynamic concept based on reflexive learning, experience, and change. In this understanding of sustainable development, if an approach is pursued and the results are different than expected, then that approach and result become the new learning point for an adaptation into a new approach. In this way, sustainable development is constantly evolving. Reflexive learning and participation are key in the Circles approach which focuses on building sustainability from the bottom up by including all stakeholders from community members, grassroots organizers, and nonprofit organizations on up to government agencies, elected officials, and private enterprises. This dynamic, reflexive approach is very similar to the pedagogy found in of indigenous epistemology.

This becomes the basis of the Circles of Sustainability, which is a four-quadrant model that identifies the social domains that most completely form a whole life: ecology, culture, politics, and economics. In this approach, diverse stakeholders from a particular place, such as a city, work together to collect data, share experiences, and define needs within the four quadrants: ecology, culture, politics, and economics. Here the quadrants are defined:

Ecology

Access, transformation, and use of materials between social and natural realms, including human engagement with nature, ranging from the built environment to the "wilderness."

Economics

Practices, discourses, and material expressions associated with the production use and management of resources.

Politics

Practices and meanings associated with basic issues of social power as they pertain to the organization, authorization, legitimation, and regulation of a social life held in common.

Culture

Practices, discourses, and material expressions, which, over time, express the continuities and discontinuities of social meaning of a life held in common.

Each of these defined quadrants has a series of seven comparative items which are included in a sustainability analysis, resulting in a total of 28 points of comparison. An example of a comparative point in ecology is "materials and energy," which refers to availability (James 2015). Based on the social and cultural context of the study, practitioners using the Circles instrument work with community members to design the content that plugs into a scale-based survey instrument. The survey will be used to measure community members' experiences. An example of a survey question based on the materials and energy point in ecology is as follows:

> How sustainable are the following aspects of the urban area? (quadrant question)
> The availability of material resources in the broader region. (point question)
> critical, bad, unsatisfactory, basic, satisfactory, good, vibrant (response choices: a scale of 1–7) (James 2015, p. 173)

These surveys are then brought out to the community and administered to members by trained surveyors from the same community. Having the surveyors being from the communities surveyed is important for building trust and understanding the context of the survey within the community, especially in a multicultural setting. The information is gathered via a Likert scale model with participants ranking satisfaction on a scale of 1–7. In another example of a Circles questionnaire, participants are asked to indicate to what extent they "agree or disagree" with a series of statements. There is a range of responses from "strongly agree: 5 to strongly disagree: 1" (James 2015, p. 175). One question is as follows: "Wealth is distributed widely enough to allow all people in our locality to enjoy a good standard of living" (James 2015, p. 175). The average of all responses is calculated as a single score and mapped on the Circles' economics quadrant in the category of "wealth and distribution" (James 2015). If the people surveyed felt there was a good distribution of wealth in their community, then the circle would be full. If not, it would have a smaller shaded area.

When measuring people's perceptions of their environments one gets a more accurate reading of their overall satisfaction. This is important in sustainability studies where many different things can impact one's immediate and long-term well-being in many different ways. For example, a person can have a high income and excellent health care but live in a contaminated environment that negatively affects their health. In a study just looking at income and healthcare access, this person might appear well-off. However, if asked, they report not feeling very well at all. Other Circles' questions follow the same pattern of asking participants about their levels of satisfaction with education, transportation, safety, access to resources, meaningful work, the state of their natural environment, and more (James 2015).

The result is a mapping of community needs and opportunities within a specific space that emphasizes the interconnectivity of economic, ecological, political (social), and cultural dimensions (James 2015). While administering the questionnaire, additional demographic data can be collected for later comparative analysis. This includes age, gender, education, place lived, size of household, income, health, ethnicity, religion, and length of time living at a location. The graphic of the mapped out Circles model provides a quick, comparative overview of strengths and weaknesses of a region's overall reported satisfaction with elements of sustainability. Demographic data provides important insights and understanding as responses are broken down and differences emerge.

Circles of Sustainability—A Personal Story

I discovered Circles of Sustainability and soon become a fellow on the project in 2014 when, as a US Fulbright scholar, I sought research tools for a comparative study of sustainability in Bolivian quinoa production. A colleague suggested I read Paul James' book, *Urban Sustainability in Theory and Practice*, and in doing so I knew I had found the tool I was looking for. Circles of Sustainability resonated with me for two reasons. First, the quadrants were amazingly similar to the four points in the Suma Qamana Andean Cross model. This meant that the communities of rural quinoa growers I was getting ready to study would be able to relate to this model and participate comfortably in the survey process. Culturally it was a good match. The second reason I chose to work with the Circles of Sustainability was that there was already a body of knowledge associated with the project so a comparative study of the Bolivian experience could be realized.

Up until 2014, Circles of Sustainability had been used exclusively in urban situations to define the complex dynamics of cities. However, I believed rural areas also had their own dynamics and boundaries that informed sustainability and lent itself to similar study. I contacted the Circles team and they agreed to support my use of the model in the first rural Circles study. The results were illuminating. My quinoa studies using Circles of Sustainability challenged sustainable development assumptions about the role of institutions, gender, and economics in well-being and particularly highlighted the impact that education and culture had on people's self-determination and creation of sustainability (Stenn 2015). For example, it was largely believed that well-being was influenced by government support and higher earnings. However, using the Circles model, I discovered that education and the ability to organize had a more direct impact on people's well-being than money and infrastructure. This was important in because it led to new ways of thinking about sustainability and highlighted the importance of accessible, high-quality education. Other organizations also had similar experiences. A new way of envisioning transportation emerged from a Circles study in Johannesburg, South Africa, and the development, placement, and use of open space was reimagined after a Circles study was conducted in Port Moresby, New Guinea (James 2015). The Circles of Sustainability is not just an assessment tool but one that uncovers needs, identifies opportunities, and can bring about positive change.

Based on this experience, I suspected that using Circles of Sustainability when assessing business environments would create new ways in which to envision sustainable business interactions, but not through surveys. Smaller business environments were too close and personal to warrant a survey, and surveys also did not seem to fit well with an agile, fast-paced business environment. The benefit I saw the Circles model bringing businesses was the identification and definition of the elements in the four quadrants that the Circles project had identified as being needed for sustainability. This next section explains what these four quadrants are and how they can be imagined in a business context. Later I will merge these quadrants with the humanistic IK model of Suma Qamana to create the SL and then show how the lens works with the BMC to grow innovation, creativity, and opportunities while building healthy, sustainable businesses.

Defining Circles of Sustainability

Ecology

Ecology, the first social domain, is about resources and how they are used. It explores the intersection between the social and natural realms and it includes the full spectrum of environmental conditions, from relatively untransformed wilderness areas to profoundly modified build environments (James 2015). More specifically, ecology examines materials, energy, water, air, flora, fauna, habitat, settlements, structures, transportation, sustenance, emissions, and waste (James 2015). This is important because rarely are all of these elements together taken into consideration in traditional business environments. In the Circles model, the source of the energy, the impact of its creation, and the results of its use are measured as are the sources of all materials used in production and their impact on workers who extract and assemble them. Structures are also measured with a look at the impact of construction and maintenance on local environments and community. In addition, environmental impacts are measured, which include impacts on animals, plants, and the local ecosystems. In the business world, this is often known as product lifecycle management (PLM). However, the Circles ecology quadrant goes deeper, offering a more comprehensive approach to PLM, specifically in areas of product sourcing and energy use.

Thinking so deeply about many business aspects that are not traditionally included in assessments makes one realize the breadth of choices, decisions, impacts, and roles that one's business has in local community and shared world environments. For example, though businesses are locally based, their use of energy and materials has worldwide impacts. In my own business, KUSIKUY, a sustainable fashion brand, applying Circles thinking led us to choose to only source our yarn from Caproca in Bolivia. Caproca is a worker-owned alpaca herder cooperative that uses organic grazing methods to care for its free-range herds of native alpaca. Alpacas are hand shorn and the yarn is transported on cooperative-owned trucks to the mill for grading, cleaning, spinning, and dying. They produce high-quality alpaca yarn and share in all costs and earnings.

Other alpaca yarn mills in Bolivia and Peru buy yarn from alpaca wholesale markets and middlemen where herders are paid less for their work and are not trained in organic herding methods. This results in a cheaper, lesser quality fleece which is then mixed with acrylic and other chemically engineered fibers to create a less expensive yarn, at a higher environmental and human cost. The herders are left in poverty conditions due to the lower pay they receive for their fleece, and nonrenewable fossil fuels and energy are wasted in the acrylic production. In addition, the acrylic fiber is petroleum based and nonrenewable. Besides taking an environmental toll with extraction, transportation, and processing with the production of chemical by-products and wastewater contamination, acrylic fiber also does not break down and becomes an environmental contaminate at the end of the clothing's lifecycle. Workers exposed to acrylic fiber in clothing manufacturing have higher levels of acrylic's DMAC, *N*-methylacetamide (MMAC), in their urine (Spies et al. 1995). Additionally, other clothing companies do not have buy-back programs, making it more likely that discarded items will end up in landfills or incinerators. Burning acrylic releases highly toxic hydrogen cyanide (CDC 2015).

Other choices we have made based on the ecology quadrant and Circles thinking is the installation of solar panels on our Vermont headquarters in order to generate new energy to replace the energy we have used to power the website, storage, and shipping that supports sales and distribution. In Bolivia, we make sure producers are using renewable hydroelectric and solar energy, we maintain our commitment to hand labor, rather than mechanized production to honor traditions of the women and also to minimize our environmental impact. We also use more strategized bulk shipping methods for product distribution to minimize the amount of resources used for delivery.

Following Circles thinking is not always easy, nor the most efficient in business terms. Our commitment to only use ethically sourced yarn limits the type of product we can produce, increases materials costs, and gives us the extra burden of educating our audience about our choice in thins and our sustainability commitment. However, it is part of a larger way of understanding our community, environment, and impact and gives us comfort to know that we are doing our best to respect and use resources wisely by carefully creating meaningful and needed products that leave a better world for future generations. There is a market for these products too as consumer consciousness is raised and people play a more active role in determining the shape of our collective future based on present-day buying choices. In this way, the KUSIKUY story is as important as the KUSIKUY Circles choices.

Culture

The next social domain, culture, when applied to a business environment becomes about the people and place where a product or service is generated. Practices, discourses, and material expressions associated with the production, use, and management of resources are emphasized and power becomes important here, with one having power over another through the use of resources and direction of production (James 2015). More specifically, culture takes into account identity, engagement, creativity, recreation, memory, projection, belief, meaning, gender, generations, inquiry, learning, well-being, and health applied to a business environment (James 2015). Again, this takes one beyond traditional day-to-day considerations in a business and focuses more on the businesses' relationship and role in a community and society. It looks at how people are able to live the lives they have reason to value, a realm deeply studied by Nobel Laureate economist, Amartya Sen.

Sen looks at restrictions that inhibit people from realizing their full lives; barriers such as gender discrimination, a lack of democratic process, limited or no access to education, and unsafe or unclean natural environments (Sen 2009). From this, he developed the Capabilities Approach which is a way of understanding justice where opportunities for one to improve their situation were balanced with their capability to do so (Sen 2009). Justice, in Sen's use of the word, is a movement toward sustainability where balanced systems of access and distribution prevail.

So to apply Sen's Capabilities Approach to the business world, if for example, one had an opportunity to sell goods—the market and demand existed and they wanted to enter this market but were unable to because of their gender, a lack of education, training, access to capital, or an unsafe or corrupt business environment—then one could not realize this opportunity. They lacked the capability to do so. According to Sen, one could also have capabilities; be well prepared with credit, investment, resources, and finished goods but not have the opportunity to enter the market because of constraints caused by gender, social status, a lack of education, and unsafe or corrupt business environments (Sen 2009). This again results in a failure in realizing justice. In both scenarios, the individual was restricted from being able to lead the life they had reason to value. This disconnect between opportunity and capability, explained Sen, is where justice fails. To grow justice, capabilities and opportunities need to work together.

This idea of justice where the opportunity to pursue a better option exists along with the skills, permissions, and the ability to do so (capabilities) is a core element of sustainable enterprises.

Like in ecology, to build sustainability, these concepts must be understood both internally as capabilities and opportunities are expanded for employees themselves, and externally as decisions are made in sourcing product, contracting out work, and influencing the policies in the environment in which the business operates. For example, an innovative, well-managed company such as Apple, which has a positive corporate culture that invests richly into employee learning and development, equal opportunity, benefits, and fair wages for its employees, yet contracts out production to foreign factories such as Foxconn in China—where people feel exploited and hopeless, commit suicide, die in industrial accidents, and improperly dispose of chemical waste from production causing permanent environmental damage—is not sustainable (Duhigg and Barboza 2012). Through its suppliers, the company is supporting the loss of others' opportunities and capabilities. Sustainability involves everyone as we all live as a single species on a single planet with finite resources. One person's actions affect another's. For example, the exploited foreign workers are underpaid and overworked, living in dormitories and unable to interact with and support their families (Duhigg and Barboza 2012). The result is families and children whose futures are negatively impacted. If opportunity is cut from one person to aid the gain for another, there is an instability created which ultimately is not sustainable.

As stated previously, the culture quadrant pertains to identity, engagement, creativity, recreation, memory, projection, belief, meaning, gender, generations, inquiry, learning, well-being, and health. Many of these areas such as memory, projection, and belief (or spirituality) are not considered to be a part of traditional business environments. However, when experimenting with culture in a business model, striving to manifest this in my own business, KUSIKUY, I was amazed at the shift it created in how values and beliefs were understood and presented as a company. KUSIKUY is largely a branding and distribution operation that, like many companies, contracts out its production to current and former LDC, the poorest and weakest segment of the international community. This creates a competitive advantage in more developed markets because of the access to skilled labor and low wages that LDCs provide. Wanting to build cultural sustainability both internally and externally, KUSIKUY workers and contractors began creating space for and encouraging creativity, recognizing our ancestors and the contributions they made to bring us to where we were today, making a timeline of events people remembered from their time at KUSIKUY, and listening to each other's personal hopes and dreams.

This led to a shift internally as deeper trust was built, greater understanding took place, and we slowed down to create a more supportive, honest work environment, where people could be respected for who they were and individuals were better known. We used team building, workshops, and tools such as Myers–Briggs personality assessments and vision boards depicting personal hopes and dreams to support this.

Perhaps even more importantly, this way of thinking culturally about a business opened up our relationships much more deeply with our outsourced production, creating additional competitive advantages which helped raise our bottom line, growing sales, and improving our product. For example, rather than quickly visiting our producers to deliver and review orders, we took the time to really get to know them. The result was the development of our best-selling product, the glitten, a multiuse fingerless glove with a cap, which the women who produce our goods created themselves, based on their years of careful observation of human behavior and knowledge of knitting. In addition, we were able to weave their culture and belief system, ancestor worship, and ceremony including their recognition and thanking of the Pachamama (earth mother), mountains and rivers, into our work. Now every KUSIKUY product comes with the tagline "Blessed with a ch'alla," which recognizes the women's habit of blessing each product as they knit it, both individually and together as a group in monthly ceremony. Our relationship with the producers is closer too, as the women say they feel more comfortable working with us—we are more like family members rather than just foreign buyers.

In a business sense, my interpretation of the culture quadrant relates to both the surrounding culture of its external environment and the culture the business creates for itself internally. These can be very different from each other but both must be taken into account for greater sustainability. For example, the company Equal Exchange, based out of Boston, Massachusetts, operates in a highly competitive capitalist, profit-driven model of private enterprise (Equal Exchange 2016). The organization deeply values worker rights, democratic decision making, and community. It operates as a worker-owned cooperative with workers having input in how prices are set, profits invested, work hours and compensation determined, volunteerism supported, and learning and development realized (Equal Exchange 2016). Specifically, each Equal Exchange worker-owner has: “the right to vote (one vote per employee, not per share); the right to serve as leader (i.e. board director); the right to information; the right to speak your mind” (Equal Exchange 2016). These are core values of Equal Exchange’s own internal culture which differ from the efficiency-driven approaches of other Boston-based or US businesses.

Politics

The next social domain, politics, as imagined in a business environment becomes about policy, rules, and regulations both internally and externally. It emphasizes practices and meanings associated with basic issues of social power in relation to the organization, authority, and regulation of a common social life (James 2015). More specifically, it encompasses organizational structure, governance, law, justice (rules and consequences), communication, critique, representation, negotiation, security, accord, dialogue, reconciliation, ethics, and accountability (James 2015).

Granted most businesses have little interest, control, or influence in governance, laws, rules, and regulations—external politics—but external politics directly impact a businesses’ ability to be sustainable. For example, if loose government oversight resulted in an old manufacturing plant contaminating the groundwater with toxic chemicals, as recently happened in North Bennington, Vermont, then that would negatively impact one’s well-being as alternative water sources for operations and staff would need to be found or purchased and health concerns arose (Yee 2016). The management of large corporations realizes the importance of having favorable external politics to support growth and development. In 2014 alone, corporations spent an estimated $2.6 billion of dollars on lobbying efforts to ensure state and national representatives favorably addressed their interests (Bump 2015). There exists an entire industry of associations funded by firms to perform research and advocate for their needs and views. Besides lobbying and association memberships, internal business policies can influence external politics.

Most importantly, the political sphere of the Circles of Sustainability when imagined in a business sense is not only about who has power and how it is used to support business interests but also how it is working to create environments where collectively solutions can be found that benefit all. Communication, critique, representation, negotiation, security, accord, dialogue, reconciliation, ethics, and accountability are also significant parts of Circles politics (James 2015). These parts led to greater transparency in business transactions where internal information and decisions are openly shared with stakeholders. This includes information on price structure and production.

My doctoral and postdoctoral research into women's well-being in the Fair Trade industry of LDCs showed that transparency was one of the most important elements in growing a more just business environment (Stenn 2013). Transparency becomes more of a democratic process through the sharing power and influence with all who are impacted by the business both directly, as the workforce, and indirectly as suppliers, contractors, customers, and local community members. Transparency is manifest in the full disclosure of costs and processes to all levels of production from supplier to worker to customer with the inclusion of feedback mechanisms so all can participate in the conversation. This may seem counterintuitive for a business. Traditionally businesses are taught to guard their corporate secrets, not disclose vendor information, costs, or designs for fear of corporate espionage and the loss of competitive advantage.

However, times are changing. With social media making it easier to share data, customers demanding more information, and organizations such as WikiLeaks disclosing private data, businesses are finding that secrecy is much harder to maintain. By building transparency and communication in an organization, departments work together more openly for the ultimate benefit of all. This type of sharing requires a relinquishing of power and building of trust. Even today full costs are hidden from the public as well as full earnings from contractors. The traditional belief is that if the consumer knew exactly how much a product was marked up from its production cost they would demand a lower price for it and the worker would want more pay once they learned what the final price of their production was. However, it can be argued that with proper education and honesty, providing transparency in pricing leads to better employee morale, contractor relations, and customer loyalty.

For example online clothier, Everlane.com, uses transparency in its pricing and production. For each item they carry, they share information on where it is produced in private, outsourced factories around the world, the costs for materials, labor, shipping, duties, and their own markups as a US-based company (Everlane.com 2016). They also design with longevity in mind, making clothing that lasts for years with timeless styles and neutral colors (Everlane.com 2016). The result is a high-quality product with a strong and growing online consumer base. Michael Preysman, CEO of Everlane, told Business Insider, "We're not going to be the cheapest price, but we won't be the most expensive either. The clothing will be Barney's quality at one-third the price" (Schlossberg 2015).

In my own social enterprise, KUSIKUY, I regularly go over production costs with the knitters we contract so together we can best strategize product and design. For example, we look at bulk costs of materials, how separate producer groups can buy yarn together, the cost of US trade shows, possibility of label production in Bolivia, where product assembly can take place, how the product is packaged and delivered in the most cost-effective and environmentally friendly way. The women understand the high cost of marketing, trade shows, and US salaries and rents. The result is that there is no longer the sarcastic resentment and questioning, "Is Fair Trade fair?" which was the inspiration for a decade of research into business sustainability and ethics. Instead, there is more of a respectful collaboration. Today we understand, think proactively, discuss, argue (critique and negotiate), and share our hopes and dreams. The result is an expansion of projects and services that KUSIKUY brings to production. When empowered to ask us, "why do you arrive here with empty suitcases?" the producers began thinking of ways in which they could be filled. Now KUSIKUY parterres with the US NGO, Reader to Reader, to make sure that suitcases are filled with books and computers every time a trip is made to Bolivia. While working with producers we noticed their college-aged children using smartphones and begin exploring how social media can be used to build more direct relationships between consumers and producers.

Outside of outsourcing and consumer relations, sustainable business politics are also about internal communication, critique, representation, negotiation, security, accord, dialogue, reconciliation, ethics, and accountability. An example of this can be seen through the experience of Brazilian, Ricardo Semler and his transnational corporation, SEMCO. Semler, the son of a post-WWII industrialist, sought to build more political sustainability within his organization through "employee-friendly radical corporate democracy" (Semler 2004). This means that employees set their own salaries, workflows, projects, teams, hiring and collectively managed costs and earnings. The result is an innovative, agile, diverse workplace that provides an average 46% return on investment and was buoyant throughout Brazil's 1990s financial crisis (Semco 2016).

As one moves along the Sustainability Circle, a pattern is starting to emerge in the ebb and flow of internal and external processes, the thinking, and planning of things immediate and also things further away both in time and space, and the scope in which businesses influence the world. At times, sustainability can seem like Edward Lorenz's Butterfly Effect, the story of the butterfly whose wing beat caused a soft puff of air which carried on the currents led to the eventual development of a tremendous storm and hurricane, showing that small causes can have large effects (Bradley 2010). But it also shows that by taking the care to build relationships and invite participation, risks, and benefits can be successfully shared by all.

Economics

The last social domain, economics, as imagined in a business environment is about production, resourcing, exchange, transfer, accounting, regulations, consumption, use, labor, welfare, technology, infrastructure, wealth, and distribution (James 2015). It emphasizes the practices, discourses, and material expressions associated with the production, use, and management of resources whether human, intellectual, or material (James 2015). These can seem to have some overlap with politics in its nod toward regulation and also ecology in its concern about resource use, but it is different in that it is also about the valuation of these resources.

Economics is often associated with scarcity and efficiency with business leaders trying to get the greatest return with limited inputs. However, inefficiency, diversity, and abundance can also be present in economics and lead to even more successful outcomes. By looking at consumption and exchange in a spirit of shared use with the goal of creatively meeting the needs of all, new ways of realizing economic success and welfare arise.

Social solidarity economy is a global approach to economics that goes beyond simple monetary exchange to value volunteerism, cooperatives, barter, community, and the natural environment. In doing so, it builds resilience, diversity, and abundance—elements needed for sustainability. Nothing is sustainable if it is going to be used up or hoarded by a few.

Reimaging labor being tied to welfare and not just efficiency led to a complete change of KUSIKUY's way of operating. Traditionally we strove to provide the most product for the lowest costs, selling our product first on value. However, over time, this led to the producers and myself becoming exhausted as sales continued to grow more than $500,000 though per unit earnings for all were kept low. Upon exploring economic sustainability more deeply, I decided to take a risk and change our organizational and cost structure. No longer focused on financial value, we instead looked at longevity and personal value. We doubled our prices, including production costs, put a 5-year guarantee on our work, and limited our production to a pre-set amount each season. This way, producers could work more slowly, taking extreme care with their work, know exactly what they would be producing so they could plan out the season, pace their work schedule and product earnings while still making a living wage.

Rather than having to knit eight pairs of gloves in a week to earn a living wage, they could now earn the same wage knitting just five. In theory, we would sell less product, though without negatively impacting earnings and building a higher quality of life for all. In addition to the 5-year guarantee and limited edition production, we provided extreme transparency to consumers disclosing product sourcing, costs, and markups as well as offering a buyback program where unwanted product could be returned for a generous store credit. These returned products are then up-cycled into sweaters and blankets for Bolivia's orphans.

Besides focusing solely on economic representation, we also looked at the producers' well-being. When the company first started, the decision was made to focus solely on rural production paid by the piece. This enabled us to provide an economic livelihood for those with the least opportunity without forcing them to give up their rural traditions for urban living (and factory work). Though logistically more complicated to manage, the "home cottage" approach has proven to be of great economic advantage, as we are now one of a few companies still specializing in handknit alpaca and are able to produce intricately designed pieces with many colors because of this. We also have a very dedicated flexible workforce which is able to expand and shrink with our orders, thus reducing overhead and stress brought about by factory work that has extensive preset costs and labor expectations.

These systems can be modeled in business economics too. For example, at KUSIKUY, alpaca fiber is transformed into alpaca clothing for exchange. By expanding one's understanding of exchange beyond currency, more sustainability and resilience is built into our company. For example, KUSIKUY is a member of IMS Barter, the largest national barter network in the United States with 16,000 members who for 30 years have been trading goods and services—without a monetary exchange, other than a nominal service fee (IMS Barter 2016). Sweaters in this sense become a direct means of exchange and are traded at full retail value for high-quality

Fig. 1.1 The sustainability lens (Stenn.)

trade show booth graphics, web design, and marketing that KUSIKUY would not have been able to afford if they could only us currency as an exchange.

Economics from a Circles perspective is also about wealth and distribution. The more evenly wealth and goods are distributed, the less disruptive things are. The International Monetary Fund is recognizing a growing worldwide phenomenon of economic inequality which President Obama has called the "defining challenge of our time." Economic inequality slows growth, destabilizes economies, concentrates power, and raises crisis risks (Dabla-Norris et al. 2015). Executive pay is an area where there is much inequality in the business world. The ratio of CEO pay to median pay within an organization is 300:1 meaning that some workers barely earn a living wage while executives at the same company earn millions of dollars (Noguchi 2015). Organizations with sustainability commitments such as certified B Corps cap their pay ratio at 5:1–10:1, meaning top executive salaries are never paid more than five to ten times higher than that of the lowest paid worker

(B Corps 2016). A B Corp is a private company that voluntarily commits to many of the principles presented in the Circles of Sustainability model via a voluntary assessment they undergo themselves. As of April 2016, there were 1704 certified B Corps across 130 industries in 50 countries (B Corps 2016). While a lack of adherence to the Circles model does not mean a company is on a guaranteed track to failure and obsolescence, it does show where vulnerabilities lie and improvements can be made (Fig. 1.1).

CHAPTER 2

Four Quadrants of Sustainability

Abstract This chapter explains in detail with case study examples, what each other the four quadrants of the sustainability lens (SL) are and how they can be understood and realized in today's business environment. The four SL quadrants are resources—where things come from: health—impact and engagement; policy—advocacy and influence; and exchange—accessibility and distribution.

Keywords Sustainability lens · Empowerment · Resources · Health policy · Exchange · Patagonia · Fair trade · Organic

Suma Qamana—A Critical Summary

The Suma Qamana model of sustainability is significant in that it decolonizes knowledge, enabling the new way of looking at the world and our relationship with it to emerge; teaches back from common indigenous origins; and offers a deep, fully humanistic understanding of sustainability. Its emphasis on "life in its glorious natural existence" is present throughout renditions of Suma Qamana from one country to the other with "harmony" being the pillar to which the concept is attached (Sanchez 2013, p. 3). Suma Qamana goes back to our common core as human beings, a single species on a single planet. Through that universal, uniform connection, it builds on our collective need for knowledge, love, action, and power, both as individuals and as a planetary species. In this sense,

T.L. Stenn, *Social Entrepreneurship as Sustainable Development*,
DOI 10.1007/978-3-319-48060-2_2

there are no "others," it is all about us as a unified being. In the same sense, what happens to one of us affects all of us through our planetary connection.

For example, if one community is doing very well and realizing many of its sustainability goals, perhaps having strong community representation, a healthy natural environment, an even distribution of wealth, and a place of belonging and respect for all community members but a neighboring community is struggling—perhaps they have a failed industrial plant contaminating their land, a lack of access to good jobs, and a low community morale. This too will affect the sustainability of the thriving neighbor. It is because people may leave the struggling community and come to the thriving one in search of better opportunity, or they may steal from or attack the thriving community or the contamination may leak into the groundwater and spread to the thriving community. In this way, we are all vulnerable and all connected. If one community (or country) is doing well and another is not then the better off community is actually not so better off.

In Suma Qamana, sustainability is grown in concentric circles with parts overlapping and impacting each other's well-being on a family, neighbor, community, municipality, state, and country level. The same principles and rules apply to all. It is believed with this model that in order for real sustainability to be achieved, in order for a viable future be secured for our children and our children's children and for many generations yet to come, we must all work together as equals on this planet and thrive not for the "good life"—defined as having the competitive advantage with the best and more than anyone else—but instead thrive to "live good," to have a shared level of well-being that permeates all and is shared universally (Huanacuni Mamani 2010). John F. Kennedy once said about economic development, "a rising tide lifts all boats," meaning that if policies or practices benefit one, others benefit from it as well (Kennedy 1960). This is the essence of Suma Qamana sustainability as well, as we in our own way strive to become more sustainable and in doing so we positively impact the sustainability of those around us as well.

However, while Suma Qamana brings an important universal perspective to sustainability, it does not bring specific day-to-day meaning to it. It has been found to be aspirational and very open to interpretation. While the theory and concepts resonate and make sense, how to actually interpret and implement them becomes difficult. This at times leads to the appearance of Suma Qamana being used to manipulate policy or deliver false promises. For example, in Bolivia Suma Qamana was an important part of the National Development Plan, the new constitution, and the Law of Mother Earth. It addressed the country's desire to move from individualized understandings of well-being to collective ones but did not enable the government, for example, to overcome the conflict between (unsustainable) growth-driven approaches and sustainability (Artaraz and Calestani 2014). Moreover, understandings of the concept are constantly being negotiated and transformed, showing the need for an understanding of it that is rooted in people's practices and beliefs rather than in theoretical constructions (Artaraz and Calestani 2014).

This is where the partnering of Suma Qamana with Circles of Sustainability becomes important. Circles gives Suma Qamana the structure it needs in which to be succinctly realized. Creating structure and applying it more narrowly to business—something that is collective, agile and able to respond to change—create the macro-environment needed for sustainability to first take root.

Circles of Sustainability—a Critical Summary

The Circles of Sustainability model is significant in that it clearly defines the multiple aspects of sustainability, forms a common language, and provides a tool for the quantitative and comparative analysis of well-being. It takes a very practical approach toward creating a global dialogue on what is important to recognize, measure, and include when considering the future of our planet and ourselves, one place at a time. The global nature of the development and use of the Circles model is also significant. As of 2016, it had been used in at least eight different countries and scores of cities with results being far-reaching and essential in bringing together different parties to work on similar issues, build coalitions, grow cooperation, understand, and collaborate—both in the assessment stage and in analysis and subsequent actions developed in response to findings.

For example in 2000 more than 1000 residents were living the inner-city Vila Chocolatão slum in Porto Alegre, Brazil, essentially working and living in the vast garbage dump (James 2015). It was dangerous, unhealthy, and the government wanted the settlement moved. Instead of forcibly moving the residents by bulldozing their shacks as is common practice, the Vila Chocolatão Sustainability Network was formed instead. Comprised of slum residents, government agencies, federal forces, nonprofit organizations, and private corporations, this Network used the Circles model to better understand the situation, collectively discover other options, and map out a long-lasting, sustainable plan. By 2006, a solution had been found. Residencial Nova Chocolatão opened up outside of the dangerous dump with recycling depots and a formal recycling sorting facility to link residents to the garbage collection process of the city. By 2011, the slum residents from the dump had completely populated the new site which also had health centers and schools (James 2015). It was a win-win for all—the government got the residents out of the dump, the residents had a more healthy life, and their children had a viable future with schools and health care, and the city had better trash collection and recycling.

Originally developed for the study of urban settings, in 2014, I applied the Circles model to rural environments through Fulbright research in the Bolivia quinoa industry with excellent results. Previously unrecognized differences from different rural communities arose, driven not by economic differences but instead by people's political cohesiveness and feelings of empowerment. For example, the wealthiest community with the greatest opportunities and access to resources surprisingly had the lowest sustainability measures. Looking at the data it was realized that this was due to divisions and mistrust associated with a long history of political strife. In my research, the Circles model showed that environmental and market stressors were not as significant as expected and that participants showed a degree of resilience and long-term thinking that was not previously recognized. In addition, the impact of education on positive development became apparent as a result of this study (Stenn 2015).

However, not all experiences with the Circles model have been as clear or successful. The model at times has been criticized as burdensome to wield, time-consuming, and needing specific expertise to use. Though used in cities, municipalities, and by nonprofit organizations, it has not been used by businesses or corporations other than FujiXerox who used it on a materiality process. The resulting FujiXerox sustainability report had interesting results but it is unclear if they made a lasting impact (Fuji Xerox 2013).

Since 2014, I have been working with university students to apply aspects of the Circles model to private businesses to identify ways in which sustainability can be more deeply recognized within their organizations. Results varied depending on the company and its industry. Often new ways of looking at the company and its relationships with suppliers, the community, and natural environment emerged.

While the Circles model offers a quantifiable, universal approach toward building a common language, values, and goals around sustainability, it lacks the depth of human emotion, the human condition, and ancestral roots in its day-to-day interpretation of sustainability. This lack of deep human connection could lead to the Circles model becoming overly prescriptive and fall into the realm of yet another certification process or product life cycle management (PLM) tool. It could also be too easily applied to situations without getting more deeply into the undercurrents of what is affecting a place and the people who engage with it. However, combining the concise infrastructure and points of action that the Circles model brings to Suma Qamana's deeply humanistic approach creates a dynamic, practical, grounded model that both addresses practical day-to-day decisions and actions while recognizing an interconnected humanity with needs, hopes, and dreams. The four quadrants of the Circles model correlate with the four points of Suma Qamana, creating a deeper, more balanced way of understanding sustainability. Juxtaposing these two models on one another creates the sustainability lens (SL).

Introducing the Sustainability Lens

Like a detective using a magnifying glass to look for clues in a crime scene, the SL uncovers clues as to how and where more sustainability can be built into an enterprise. It is a combination of two models of sustainability: Suma Qamana indigenous ways of being and Circles of Sustainability place-based assessment. Suma Qamana and Circles are both quadrant models meaning they have four fields in them. I have aligned them to create a new combined way of viewing and experiencing sustainability. The result is transformative. It is no longer a human versus logistic view or one that is an A+B approach of each, rather it a new synergistic rendering of both. It also becomes an active model used to facilitate change and build sustainability, not simply assess it. It involves creativity, taking the time to ask hard questions and a commitment to building innovative solutions. Some solutions may be amazingly easy, others very complex needing to be slowly built and implemented over time. And it is not all bad news, businesses are often surprised by how much innovation and sustainability they already have built into their practices and new ideas illuminated by the SL often end up being money savers, money makers, or improvements over what is currently being done.

Once the SL is used, "to do" items become visible. These can be prioritized, strategized, and promoted, strengthening the company's practices, products, impact, and reputation. The SL creates great storytelling and marketing moments helping businesses to build their "unique selling point" and set themselves apart from the competition. The SL also helps businesses to align more with community thereby building a more solid client base, happier employees, and mutually beneficial partnerships.

The following is a detailed explanation of the facets of the lens and how they work. In the next section of this book, I will show how the SL can be used with popular business design tools such as Business Model Canvas, to reimagine enterprises.

The Sustainability Lens—An Overview

> Engaging the Sustainability Lens is not an altruist task of endless work, an imposed model or costly membership that does not exactly fit, rather it's a fun, creative, interactive, empowering way to strengthen one's business that is neither tedious nor boring and can quickly produce amazing results.
>
> — (T. Stenn, founder of the Sustainability Lens)

Resources: Where Things Come From

Actively seek the best sources for energy, materials, and production to minimize a business impact on ecosystems and maximize the benefits one brings to people and the planet. Includes supply chain management for self and suppliers, sourcing of raw materials down to the very soil it comes out of, managing waste and the product's life cycle through active, ongoing research, and query.

Health: Impact and Engagement

Build love in a business through customer, contractor, and employee relations, celebrations, transparency, and trust. Democratically engage all (customer, contractor, and employee) in decision making and strategizing. Strive to ensure that all are able to live the life they have reason to value by seeking ways to build opportunities and capabilities.

Policy: Advocacy and Influence

Actively model and advocate for changes needed for greater sustainability through internal business policies and external influences from supplier selection, production, profits, and investment to community involvement. Participate in dialogue and be open to different ideas.

Exchange: Accessibility and Distribution

Seek to diversify methods of exchange through barter, volunteerism, cooperatives, profit sharing, local currencies, time trades, and closed-loop lending. Monitor the speed and pace of the business to ensure that exchanges are more equal and growth is steady.

As the lens is moved over different elements of business development and everyday management, new ways in which to approach these tasks emerge.

The Details Explained

Lens Facet—Resources

Resources is a combination of Suma Qamana's Yachay knowing and Circles' ecology. The result is a proactive view of how and where things come from. Similar to PLM, the process of managing the entire life cycle of a product from inception, through engineering design and manufacture, to service and disposal of manufactured products, resources, as seen through the SL, examines supply chains all of the way back to the earth that a raw material emerged from as a plant animal or mineral and looks at the human hands and processes it underwent to get to one's business. This includes energy, transportation, working conditions, byproducts, waste, and disposal along the entire supply chain, even that of contractors and suppliers. Contractors' and suppliers' supply chains are important because when a business purchases goods or services, they are also supporting and encouraging the conditions and situations that created it. Because of this, businesses have tremendous power and influence through their buying decisions and operation choices. By asking suppliers about their practices, awareness of sustainability is shared. Requiring that suppliers have sustainable practices in their production helps to grow and strengthen sustainability. This becomes exponential as suppliers then have to go back to their suppliers to enquire about their sustainability practices as well. This inquiry helps to inform other businesses about more holistic ways to view their materials sourcing and production. Queries like this lead to greater sustainability across industries. For example as the 1992 Earth

Summit in Rio failed to produce an agreement to stop deforestation, a group of businesses, environmentalists, and community leaders came together to create the Forest Stewardship (FSC 2016). The FSC wanted to provide an alternative to massive clear-cutting that threatened animal species and native people and destroyed the natural environment, and the subsequent boycotts that followed as angry consumers learned of the plight of the land. Now operating in 20 countries, the FSC has guidelines and provides certification for responsibly managed forests that provide environmental, social, and economic benefits. Businesses such as furniture makers, lumber suppliers, and paper mills can now produce product using FSC-certified wood (FSC 2016). Consumers are educated to seek out the FSC logo. As an individual consumer, one has the same power and influence with goods and services purchased.

More specifically, Yachay is about being aware of the world around you and how it interrelates. It is about developing expertise, building skills, acquiring knowledge, and embracing diversity. It is also about opposites, transition, and balance. So as sustainability is more deeply explored and knowledge is built, Yachay gives time, space, and understanding for this as well. It does not condemn others for less sustainable practices but creates a place where people can work together for better outcomes for all.

The specific elements of Circles' ecology show where the deep Yachay inquisitiveness can be focused. It helps to more specifically define the links along the supply chain, spelling out elements such as water usage, emissions (air), landscaping (flora and fauna), and transportation.

Resources in the SL are about conservation, reuse, and justice. Conservation means that minimal resources are being used with minimal impact on the planet both through extraction and transformation. In agriculture, for example, this could include water management techniques such as drip irrigation or mulching that reduce water usage in agriculture, organic farming methods which keep harmful pesticides, herbicides, and fungicides out of the environment, and composting for soil renewal and waste reduction.

Reuse is about extending the life of resources. For example, in Bolivia nonreturnable, 2 L plastic soda bottles are cut in half and reused as light shades, planters, funnels, and scoops. Old tires are used to make shoe soles, sandals, door stops, washers, and bags while inner tubes are fashioned into wallets and patches, and used to hold things together. Our company, KUSIKUY, supports reuse through a buy-back program for used products. Customers return an item for $20 credit toward their next purchase. The used items are sent back to Bolivia where knitters make them into handknit blankets and sweaters that are donated to children in the village orphanage.

Justice takes place with the living elements of production: humans and animal resources. It is about living and working conditions, compensation, and one's overall quality of life. When working with animals, their access to a natural environment, healthy food, freshwater, and a dignified death are important. So is their environmental impact. For example, overgrazing and erosion caused by goat herds in the Andes Mountains is not sustainable, even if the animals are free range and organically raised (Lozada 1991). Goats are a nonnative species that the fragile, local environment is unable to adapt to (Lozada 1991).

Often in animal production, native species and scale make the difference between what is sustainable and what is not. Choosing sustainable options are not always the most cost-effective or the most efficient. But sustainability is not about efficiency, it is about longevity and often requires one to operate at a pace where the earth and people have time to renew and replenish themselves.

To examine resources through the SL, one does not need to be a university-level researcher, biochemist, or industry expert. There are multiple ways for discovering best practices in the use of materials and human rights and environmental violations in the supply chain. The Internet has led to widespread democratization of data. By doing a "Google Scholar" search one can find reputable, peer-reviewed studies on materials and processes. By searching a supplier's name online with "fraud" or "violation" put after it, one can discover problems suppliers have been cited for that they might not readily tell you. Yachay is about finding knowledge, not just being knowledgeable; it is an active process of inquiry and discovery. And it is not just the discovery of wrongs, but the discovery of solutions as well. Yachay encompasses all knowledge, not just that from university archives or government reports, but also knowledge from the ancestors. In the language of Transition Towns, a global movement originating in England which focuses on living in a post-oil era, the seeking of ancestral knowledge is known as "re-skilling" (Hopkins 2008). In development literature, the valuing of indigenous knowledge is directly related to one's feeling of well-being and the building of resilience (Gupta 2003). As problems are uncovered in a supply chain scrutiny re-skilling and indigenous knowledge can be sought as one looks back to how it was done before to see where forgotten, simple, practical solutions may lie.

This is not to say that modern approaches and technology are bad but that over time, simple, sustainable approaches may have been lost. Through the Yachay balance of knowledge, contradictions occur and exist as one continually discovers and moves forward to more sustainable solutions. The dynamics of opposites sought by Sam Qamana enables contradictions to be embraced and learned from.

Lens Facet—Health

Health is a combination of Suma Qamana's Munay love and Circles' culture. The result is a positive, inclusive, generous, proactive way of viewing others in relation to one's enterprise. It is about relationship and shared human culture. It includes the valuing of achievement, celebration, rest, and community. There is balance in health. One has a job and goes to work, but one's community and family, though perhaps not physically at the workplace, are also a part of that. Without family and community, there are no workers to hire and without work, there are no resources for sustaining a family or community. From the health perspective on the SL, one needs a job to support a family and a family to make life meaningful and worthwhile. So in that sense, a job becomes meaningful and worthwhile and coworkers are like family.

Circles assign several specifics to this realm including gender, recreation, learning, and health. When viewing an organization through the health facet, these parts of an individual matter. Therefore, the experience and needs for sustainable health will change from one individual to the next. For example, in Bolivia, the government recognizes a woman's extra work of cooking and caring for the family as well as participating in work outside of the home (Webber 2011). Because of this, a woman's legal work week is 35 h long before mandatory overtime is required, while a Bolivian man's legal work week is 40 h long, before mandatory overtime (Webber 2011). The extra 5 h given to women recognizes the additional work they have at home.

In production, health also involves looking toward suppliers and their practices as well as those of the business itself. Practices such as flexible work hours, sick leave for workers when they or family members fall ill, access to health care, and training and leadership opportunities are all important. Amartya Sen defined justice as an individual being able to "live the life they have reason to value" (Sen 2009). The circles' health quadrant very much supports this by promoting supportive, inclusive, worker-centric workplaces.

In the spirit of Munay love, celebration is also vitally important for sustainability. Just as nature has cycles, so do people and businesses. In Bolivia, the Andean ch'alla or monthly blessing features prominently in the business realm. Each month businesses shut early and owners and staff gather together around burning incense, being thankful for all the business has to offer, the customers, products, suppliers, earth mother, mountains, rivers, and ancestors for sustaining and not forgetting them (Goldstein 1998). Specifically, the generosity and well-being of both the ancestors and customers are celebrated as food and drink are shared. Products, animals, structures, and machines are also included in this, being recognized for their vital role in the organization's success and decorated with mistura (confetti) and blessed with beer (Goldstein 1998). Everyone and everything is celebrated together, there is no singling out of one individual over another.

A final aspect of health that is important to remember in the SL is that of multiculturalism. This refers to the ability to accept and celebrate others' cultures. Differences are tolerated in this model and, like in the Suma Qamana model, space is given for opposites and contradictions to exist.

Lens Facet—Policy

Policy is a combination of Suma Qamana's Ruray, doing, and Circles' politics. Like many of the aspects of sustainability, it has both macro- and micro-elements to it. Macro-policy relates to the type of government, laws, freedoms, and opportunities that exist within the place or nation where a business resides. Micro-policy concerns the governing and rules of the organization itself. Organizational (micro) policy can affect both the employees of an organization and the surrounding community and natural environment. Policy in the SL determines everything from which charities are supported, where donations go, which little league team is sponsored to what types of materials will be used, how waste is disposed of, and what the company rules will be. As much as health is the love, policy is the heart, the mechanism that pumps the love around the do-er, the point of action.

From a Circle perspective, policy is also about communication, reconciliation, ethics, and accountability. This is where past wrongs can be corrected and flaws, discovered through the SL, can be recognized and fixed. Often this is a difficult time for an organization. There is pressure for a company to uphold a degree of ethical oversight and a positive reputation, however over time, decisions can be made and situations arise that may seem unethical or unsustainable. Integrity continuity guidelines set standards for ethical behavior and can help to prevent unethical occurrences. However, 60 % of chief executives and boards of directors failed to engage in integrity continuity planning discussions or to include such considerations in strategic planning (Taub 2002). Although predicting ethical scandals in US businesses is not an exact science, some estimate that an average of 20 "major" business ethical misconduct disasters occurs each year. (Taub 2002). These disasters include harassment, criminal activity, financial improprieties, customer deception, bribery, regulatory violations, corruption, and undisclosed conflicts of interest (Chandler 2005).

To recognize and change these creates a degree of vulnerability; for example, a company must first admit to a wrong or an error. This can be a frightening time for a business where it seems the admittance of a wrong either by correcting it or outright acknowledging it could lead to a loss of confidence and clientele. However, the opposite is true. Integrity continuity planning is also due diligence. Ethical issues must be on the strategic agenda. No matter how horrific or deep-seated the difficulty is, companies that are proactive in acknowledging and correcting these situations fare better in the public eye in the long term than those that try to hide, overlook, or minimize a damage or wrong. In the short term admitting to an error can seem costly and unnecessary, something to be brushed under the carpet, but sustainability is about longevity. In the long term, admitting to and correcting an error often results in a stronger operation, better practices, a greater commitment from the workforce, and more loyal customers (Chandler 2005). Besides, in today's world with unlimited access to data, it is increasingly difficult for businesses to hide secrets and wrong doings. It is more favorable for a business to disclose a problem and the subsequent solution than to have the public do it for them. In conclusion, policy as a facet of the SL can be thought of as rules and governance but it is also very much public relations as these rules and governance are communicated within and outside of the organization.

Case Study—Kusikuy

KUSIKUY, a fashion brand that specializes in alpaca clothing, was founded in Bolivia in 1996. Our main supplier of alpaca sweaters was a member of Bolivia's massive informal sector, a woman who sourced our products from many, indistinguishable, family-run, back-room production facilities. These were literally a room in a house with three or four knitting looms that brothers, sisters, cousins, and neighbors would use to make medium-quality tourist-grade goods for sale in the La Paz markets. This was a good place to start and provided us access to inexpensive sweaters that were easily sold in the United States where I was attending graduate school. Having lived in Bolivia for many years and knowing the people well, we strove, through our purchasing power and product choices, to improve working conditions and product quality. In 1999, KUSIKUY was ready to become a Fair Trade company and needed to document that workers were being paid a fair wage, had a clean, safe working environment, and job security. However, with this production model, wages and working conditions were impossible to track.

KUSIKUY presented itself to the public as a natural fiber company that supported Bolivia's informal sector by creating opportunities for informal sector workers. People embraced the message and liked out products resulting in steady growth at 20 % a year. However, our moment of angst came when, as we started moving toward a more transparent Fair Trade model, we began to scrutinize costs and processes more, we noticed our materials' costs were significantly lower than other knitting groups', even though (we thought) we were sourcing the same 100 % pure alpaca fiber as they were. We tested the yarn from our informal sector producers and found that our 100 % alpaca sweaters were false—they were mixed with acrylic! Horrified we confronted the head manager of production. She admitted that she really had no control over the actual fiber being used since the KUSIKUY goods were produced alongside so many others. She had requested pure alpaca but had no way of verifying that in fact was what it was. She could not control the quality.

We could have turned a blind eye to whole things, after all, what was the chance that one of our US clients would actually do a laboratory analysis on our fiber? There were some good reasons to take this route; we had good earning on the goods. We did some research and found that if we were to switch production to formal sector, worker-owned cooperatives, and membership associations, we would be able to track all production and materials—guaranteeing a fair wage and pure alpaca. However, our production costs would triple and so would our final product price. We would lose our entire market!

We did not know about the SL yet at that time (by then it was 1999), but we did make a sustainability lens-esque decision. We would be honest and introduce our mixed alpaca to our current clientele as the new "sport alpaca" and highlight the positive attributes acrylic brought to the garment: it kept it affordable, held its shape longer, did not shrink, and was more durable. We thought we were presenting an improvement, but in fact, our audience hated it and demanded we stick with our original, "natural fiber" model—without synthetics.

That left us in a dilemma. In order to actually have the pure alpaca our customers thought they were getting, we needed to completely change our production and product or issue our own "recall" and offer to take back the "false alpaca" goods. Our informal sector producer was unable to come up with a guaranteed solution to the dilemma—because production was spread out so much, there was no way for her to guarantee the yarn quality or wages, ever.

We decided to take the product change route, and began promoting our higher quality, more expensive, handknit products—creating a gorgeous signature cable design. We started with accessories that were more accessible price wise, and expanded to baby sweaters and finally adult products. Sales dropped as customers struggled with the new price points; however, soon new customers began arriving. Eventually, high-end couture designers from New York City began contacting us for production and a whole new area of work opened for the knitters as they provided private label knitting for the designers. Through this experience, we greatly improved out handknitting skills and offerings and became a more solid, sustainable company.

This story demonstrates the policy facet of the SL. There is an action that is needed to happen and dilemmas over communication, ethics security, and accountability. Through dialogue, negotiations, and governance, KUSIKUY was able to steer through a major shift in the company, while still maintaining integrity and control. In the long term, product was improved and the company committed to a higher degree of sustainability positively impacting the lives of the handknitters. We are still in touch with our informal sector partners and occasionally provide them with technical assistance and share custom work with them when we can dictate the materials and labor used.

Lens Facet—Exchange

Exchange is one of the facets most closely associated with business. Business is often defined as the exchange of goods and services. However, as a facet of the SL, exchange is realized a bit differently. Exchange as a lens facet is a combination of Suma Qamana's Ushay, power, and Circles' economics. This is an appropriate matching up of models because those who control the buying and financial planning of a place hold much power; they clench the purse strings that fund well-being for everyone. This sounds like a potentially coercive, corrupt idea of power, though sustainability is neither coerce nor corrupt. Ushay is power in the sense of vitality, force, energy, and potential. It is the ability of the Phoenix to rise from the ashes and become something new and revitalized, though it is also reflective. It is a power that comes from years of experience which is often quietly held by the elders and only shared when asked for. Economics in the Circles model is exchange, transfer, production, distribution, and consumption. Combining these together creates space in which to question current methods and imagine how things could be approached differently, either through different materials usage, transformation processes, distribution, or changes in final deliverables.

When a company is engaged in exchange, there comes an element of education too. Ushay is power and it is the power to educate and persuade. Customers, suppliers, and workers need to know how and why a business is sustainable. They need to know why this is important and how it is different from nonsustainable practices and companies. They also need to know where nonsustainable practices are occurring and how often. Size and scale do matter. Often for people to fully understand and choose to support sustainability, they need to understand what nonsustainability is. Nonsustainable practices such as excessive use of nonrenewables; enslaved, child, and sweatshop labor; poor waste management; and environmental and human rights abuses prevail and are often unseen. Making sustainability visible is a task found in exchange. Like-minded organizations committed to sustainability can work together to share in educating the public. This is often done in the form of workshops, conferences, annual meetings, data sharing, social media, documentary films, speaker series, and testimonials.

Organizations working with the SL often are referred to as "social enterprises" or organizations with a "social mission." This is responding to the broader view that sustainability creates as one realizes that a company's existence and future lies not just within itself but within the entire community. It is in the community where customers, buyers, and suppliers come from. This community is both local and global as materials are sourced and assembled in different places and products are shipped around the world.

Taking the effort to engage in sustainability is difficult and results are not always immediately apparent. Membership organizations, such as organic certifiers, can help facilitate one's entrance into a more socially consciousness way of operation by providing framework in which to engage and explain efforts, assessments, and benchmarks for organizations to use to demonstrate progress, and a common language and community in which to strategize and engage with (Blackman and Rivera 2010). For example, the Fair Trade Federation (FTF), established in 1995, has members working with hundreds of producer groups worldwide (Stenn 2013). FTF supports many of the elements of SL including carefully sourced product with minimal environmental impact, living wages, and proper cultural interaction with producers, long-term contracts, and transparency in pricing and negotiations. Here one can find resources for their own production, finished goods to offer for sale, and a supportive environment to help with challenges faced with sustainable global production—sales, shipping, regulations, and logistics. In addition, the FTF has their own outreach programs, conferences, and materials (Stenn 2013), working together in support of Fair Trade and a step toward greater sustainability. Besides FTF there is also FT USA, Fair Trade International working on different aspects of sustainability in trade as well. These both have certifying programs and like the FTF provide logos, customer education, outreach, and promotion of the idea of Fair Trade (Stenn 2013). Having memberships and networking within these organizations helps grow and educate others on the idea of sustainability.

The Organic Trade Organization (OTA) and USDA Organic are also membership organizations and certifiers that embrace many aspects of the sustainability and provide visible logos, consumer education, and support for members (OTA 2016). Working largely in agriculture, the OTA lobbies congress for more safety and access for organic standards while also educating consumers. The Organic Consumers Association is a consumer advocacy group that is focused on creating more access and safety in agriculture, including long-term stewardship of the earth, the use of renewable in farming, and non-GMO (genetically modified organisms) crop development (OCA 2016). A B Corp as another advocacy group that educates consumers on many of the same things that the SL brings into focus such as an organization's energy use, employee policies, and materials sourcing (B Corps 2016). There are many more advocacy groups, citizen groups, membership groups that support the principles of sustainability, help build more sustainable businesses, share in educating, and reaching out to people. These include Transition Towns, Fair World Project, and Green America.

CHAPTER 3

Enhancing the Lens

Abstract This chapter brings new ideas based on economic permaculture and social solidarity economy, to illuminate, inspire, and create practical, innovative approaches in response to needs and challenges identified through the sustainability lens.

Keywords Permaculture · Social solidarity economy

Working with the sustainability lens (SL) involves first discovering ways that sustainability could be strengthened and then finding creative ways in which to grow it. Often it is difficult to imagine how this can happen, especially without any specific model or path to follow. The open flexibility the SL brings that makes it so universally appealing, relevant and far-reaching in its scope, is the same challenge it brings as one seeks solutions without really knowing what options are available. Since the SL is not prescriptive, but rather a diagnostic tool with a call to action, it is good to know where other options for building sustainability may lie.

There are two concepts that can be layered over different halves of the SL to help identify new, creative solutions to areas lacking in sustainability. These are social solidarity economy (SSE) and permaculture. Both are interdisciplinary and have been developed and promoted by a diverse, multinational, informally networked team of practitioners, nonprofit organizations, government agencies, citizen groups, academia, and private

T.L. Stenn, *Social Entrepreneurship as Sustainable Development*,
DOI 10.1007/978-3-319-48060-2_3

enterprise within the past 20 years. The concepts of SSE and permaculture are being practiced in different parts of the world on the individual, town, and municipal levels. They are growing in popularity and have produced, viable, effective solutions for building sustainability. These concepts are not a Band-Aid or out-of-pocket, one-size-fits-all solutions to sustainability, but they offer different ways of seeing things and building connections that can be adapted to grow sustainability in a locally, nationally and business environment.

SSE addresses the SL facets of policy and health. It is action based and focused on the social aspect of economics, which in its original Greek roots oikos "house" and nomos "custom" or "law," means caring for the home (Harper 2001). Social entrepreneurship (SE) brings new ways in which economic and social needs of local and international communities are met through innovative production, exchange, and consumption of goods and services (Kawano et al. 2009). RIPESS, the International and Intercontinental Network of Social SSE founded in 1997, supports the development and interpretation of SE worldwide, emphasizing the importance of global solidarity to build and strengthen an economy that puts "people and the planet front and center" (RIPESS 2016). I have been an active member of RIPESS since 2010—participating in global forums and information sharing—and have seen many innovative projects and approaches emerging from RIPESS that inspire sustainability.

Permaculture is more related to the resources and exchange facets of the SL. It examines how systems work together looking at nature patterns and design thinking for inspiration. Permaculture is largely associated with agriculture and natural landscape, but its nature-inspired design thinking can be successfully applied to nonagriculture situations too. Permaculture is about sourcing and transforming resources in a balanced, sustainable way examining how different entities support each other either directly or largely indirectly through complex relationships in the natural world (Holmgren 2002). This is very relevant to businesses which strive to create value through the transformation of a good or the production of a service. By looking for inspiration from nature's systems of transformation, new ways of businesses can interact with and transform their environment in a mutually beneficial and sustainable way.

The following chapter will introduce these two concepts in more detail. The purpose is to expand the ways in which one can approach sustainability and add more tools to the toolkit of possible approaches and solutions.

Permaculture

Permaculture, a contraction of "Permanent Agriculture," was developed by Bill Mollison and David Holmgren in Australia in the 1970s (Holmgren 2002). Permaculture originally focused on sustainable living and land use based on the observation of nature to create regenerative systems largely in agriculture and building. It has since grown to become an entire philosophy of social design stimulating creative household and community initiatives that reduce ecological footprints, increase resilience, and re-localize economies. There are three core tenets of permaculture: care of the earth, care of people, and return of surplus (Holmgren 2002). In traditional business models, surplus would indicate disequilibrium, a breakdown in supply and demand, maybe prices were too high, or not the right goods were produced. However, permaculture values restraint and giving back—taking what is needed and reinvesting the rest (Holmgren 2002). Surplus is so important in permaculture that organizations plan for this, being sure to have extra product to give back to the community. For example, farmer Paul Harlow of Harlow Farms in Westminster, Vermont, purposely overplants his 150 acres of fields so parts can be left for volunteer gleaners who collect the surplus for community distribution, via the local food shelf (Hardwick 2012). Each year, Harlow donates upward of 56,000 pounds of fresh lettuce, kale, collards, carrots, beets, peppers, broccoli, cabbage, summer squash, zucchini, winter squash, pumpkins, and more (Hardwick 2012).

Sustainability in nature is about abundance and redundancy. Looking toward nature as a model of sustainability one sees that there is not just a single bird, tree, or flower, there are many. Efficiencies would dictate that having song and beauty in a single bird would suffice. However, this also brings about tremendous risk and vulnerability. If a plague or predator affected the bird, there would be neither song nor beauty any longer. Nature favors redundancy over efficiency. In redundancy, systems differ slightly from each other so if, for example, one particular variety of bird is negatively impacted by an event or disease, there are others that still exist and may even flourish in the absence of the one. Redundancy can be built into economics too. Economic redundancy minimizes risk, expands possibilities, and changes the way in which resources are imagined. An example of economic redundancy could be multiple ways in which to access a good, perhaps through credit, cash, work, trade, or volunteerism (solutions related to SE).

Permaculture offers a way in which to refer to nature as a model or inspiration when imagining how sustainable transformations can take place in economics. For example, when defining exchanges, it is common to think simply of currency, however, as in nature, there are many different types of exchanges. If an apple tree's economic model is the dispersing of seeds to grow more trees, then this exchange takes place in several different ways; one is through the offering of nectar and flowers to bees in exchange for pollination and the other is through the offering of fruit (apples) to animals in exchange for seed dispersal. However, nature also has pollination happen on the wind and some species do not use pollination at all. At the same time, seeds can be dispersed not just by animals but also by the wind, through direct consumption (ingestion) and by opportunism (i.e., burrs that catch hold of one's garment). In nature, there are multiple means to an "economic end" resulting in more options, resiliency, innovation, flexibility, and creativity.

Other ideas that are central to permaculture include a zero waste economy—where all energy is renewable and all discarded materials are designed to become resources for others to use. The Zero Emission and Research Initiative (ZERI), an international community of thousands of committed researchers, practitioners, and policy analysts, has been working on this idea since 2004. An example of innovations members have developed is William Liang's stone paper which turns the massive amounts of dust generated by mines into 100 % recyclable paper that is tree free, consumes no water in its production, and frees up land for other uses (ZERI 2016).

Nature is also about closed-loop systems: microcosms that exist where organisms interact with each other symbiotically. For example, an apple tree produces leaves that, in the autumn, fall to the ground and are composted into fertilizer that nourishes the tree in the spring when new growth happens. Microorganisms feed on the leaves to turn them into the compost that the roots feed on. The nutrients the roots take from the compost enable the tree to make new leaves. These leaves then produce energy; the leaves age and fall off the tree, are transformed into nutrients by microorganisms and the cycle repeats. The microorganisms and tree are dependent on one another and work together in a closed-loop system.

In economics, balance is maintained through place-based closed-loop systems. However, a global economy is not local nor place based. Inequalities in exchange with production and consumption taking place out of the local community create imbalances that lead to a slowing down of the local economy. For example, if wages a local company might have spent on local production are spent on cheaper foreign production instead, the result is a loss of the local investment. A closed-loop system keeps the wages local along with consumption; people consume what they produce.

As in nature and permaculture, a local currency supports local consumption and balanced, sustainable closed-loop exchanges. A local currency, such as New York's BerkShares, is a means of exchange that has a monetary value and can be used instead of national currency for local transactions. Local currency, also supported by SSE, circulates among individuals and businesses in the local community creating closed-loop exchanges that keep earnings in one place strengthening local communities. Sometimes, as is the case of BerkShares, there is a favorable exchange rate where local currencies are valued at 5 % more than the national currency creating an exchange rate of US $95 to $1.00 BerkShare (Ellis 2012). Steffen Root, a local business owner who accepts BerkShares explained, "We can all be richer, both financially and community-wise, if we keep our money local, do our best to support our local businesses, and do as little outside sourcing as possible" (BerkShares 2016). Six years after its founding in 2006, over 3 million BerkShares had been issued (Ellis 2012). By 2016, there were over 400 local businesses accepting BerkShares (BerkShares 2016).

Continuing to look toward nature models, such as the leaf–fall cycle of trees or ideas of abundance, when pondering ways in which to grow sustainability opens one too many new opportunities that they might not have considered earlier. Some other nature-based models to consider are bees and pollination in relation to the sharing of ideas and creative resources in order to make energy or honey as in the bee's case. Another nature model that relates to long-term effects of actions would be the flow and movement of water as it transforms environments and obstacles.

Social Solidarity Economy

SSE began in Lima, Peru, in 1997 as "economia solidaria" (solidarity economy). At the same time political thinkers, economists, academics, and civil society members were developing ideas for what became known as SSE in Canada, France, and Portugal (RIPESS 2016). SSE was presented at the World Social Forum in Brazil in 2001, and the Intercontinental Networks for the Promotion of Social Solidarity Economy (RIPESS) was formed (RIPESS 2016). RIPESS is an active network of practitioners, philosophers, and academics who communicate via social media and at world conferences, sharing white papers, case studies, projects, and ideas focused on the growing of an economy that addresses social needs and forms alliances with marginalized people such as those without access to land, income, education, energy, food, or water, to ensure these needs are met and resources shared in creative and collective ways. Many of these approaches can be used to address needs or shortcomings found with the SL.

Some of SSEs ideas are similar to those found in permaculture such as that of local currencies and closed-loop environments. SSE also supports innovative approaches to ecological and cultural creation, democratic production, exchange, consumption, and surplus allocation (Miller 2013). However, though it has ecology and conservation as part of its core principles, it is not as nature based as it is community (social) based. SSE looks at diverse ways people can collectively get their needs met, going beyond traditional models of individual ownership, currency, and consumption (Kawano et al. 2009). It looks at the basic needs of a community which include education, shelter, health care, employment, food, water, and energy and sees how these can be met through the economic cycle of creation, production, exchange, use, and the allocation of surpluses. In each cycle phase, many different approaches are identified. The following section goes into more detail of the different quadrants of the SSE circle and discusses how these influence SSE in innovative and creative ways.

Creation

Creation is both ecological and cultural. It calls for the establishment of a commons; a publicly owned outdoor meeting and recreational places such as a park, promenade, or central town square. Here music and art are shared, community members socialize and exchange ideas, and a place of beauty and nature is maintained (Kawano et al. 2009). Creation also calls for the collective ownership of land and the use of community land trusts. This creative use of land creates more accessibility for the landless and encourages people to engage with the land in new and collaborative ways. For example in my Vermont community, the land trust will purchase and renovate housing that is then offered at a reduced cost mortgage to lower income families. When the houses are sold, the same low-cost mortgage is transferred to the next owner. We also have private land trusts where farmers bequeath their land for continued farm use. Here young people can set up community-sponsored agriculture programs, offering fresh produce to families who prepurchase a share in the farm and share in its harvest. They do not have the cost of purchasing the land, but they do have the land access and use.

Production

Production is about how things are made and by whom. Examples of different approaches to production include dip it yourself, where people transform materials into new uses themselves in their home environments (Kawano et al. 2009). Often this is referred to as "upcycling" as discarded materials are made into something else such as the durable, fashionable shopping bag made of crocheted discarded plastic bags. However, new materials can be used too such as yarn to knit a sweater with. Worker cooperatives where workers themselves own the means of production and make decisions and share in profits together, family-based production sometimes called cottage industry, where production is again done at home but offered for sale to outside customers, democratic employee stock ownership programs where employees can vote on company actions and all own shares in the organization, and producer cooperatives or associations, where producers form a membership network that advocated for the collective work of each of them. These are all creative alternatives to the traditional owner/worker model of production. In these alternatives, there is more participation from the worker and collective decision making.

Exchange and Transfer

This section looks at ways in which goods can be distributed. Rather than relying solely on traditional buy and sell via currency, alternative exchange methods create more diversity and reduce risk. For example, the devaluation of currency has a direct negative effect on a business that is exchanging only in currency. However, if a business is using multiple types of exchange then all is not lost with the currency devaluation, there are other types of exchange that are still strong. Some other exchange options include gifts that work well to distribute surpluses, barter clubs where goods are exchanged for other goods rather than currency, community (or local) currencies, sliding scale models where a suggest price is posted but people can pay what they feel they can afford, Fair Trade where intention and transparency are placed in the pricing model to ensure that all participants in the creation of the product are earning a dignified wage and have a good work environment, time trade where time instead of currency is exchanged via a time bank that stores people's reported hours in exchange for goods or services (Kawano et al. 2009).

Consumption

How products are consumed is also an important part of sustainability. This section is about the choices consumers and companies make when selecting which good or materials to use and purchase. The solidarity lens is already looking at the environmental and human impact of materials being used in production. Some options for consumption are consumer cooperatives where people as members get together and purchase product in bulk and distribute it into smaller quantities themselves. This results in lower costs and less packaging, which results in less waste in the landfill. Ethical purchasing is examining the supply chain to ensure that materials, energy, and labor are engaged in a respected, careful way, and self-provisioning means creating the raw materials yourself. For example, a tomato farmer who decided to create his own line of tomato sauce using his own tomatoes is self-provisioning the raw materials for his business.

Surplus

Perhaps the most important and least recognized part of a business is the managing of surplus. This can have a tremendous effect on sustainability, use of resources, and health of one's company and the community. Under SE there are many options to surplus, which may take the form of goods or currency. There is the composting and reuse of byproducts from production, the donation of excess goods, or liquidation of old inventory for distribution along more economically accessible routes. There are also many creative ways for financing to take place. Excess capital can be put into credit unions where the community is a member of the bank themselves and jointly make decisions together as to loans and interest rates. There is community financing where members gift funds to each other for a larger investment and impact and social investment funds where people purposely choose to invest in companies with social missions.

Socially responsible investing (SRI) targets businesses with environmental, social, and corporate governance criteria that generate long-term financial returns and positive societal impacts (Woll 2015). SRI is on the rise as social enterprises tend to be innovation pioneers with 59 %

introducing a new product or service in the last 12 months alone with good results—in the United Kingdom alone, 40 % more social enterprises were growing compared to mainstream small- to medium-sized enterprises with 50 % reporting a profit and 26 % breaking even (Villenueve-Smith and Temple 2015). SRI as investments were valued at $6.57 trillion in 2014 (Woll 2015).

CHAPTER 4

Focus on the Business Model Canvas

Abstract This chapter introduces the Business Model Canvas (BMC), an open-source, design-thinking tool. In step-by-step detail, each of the four quadrants of the sustainability lens is applied to the nine sections of the BMC, creating an array of 36 different angles and approaches for enterprises to imagine and realize sustainable development.

Keywords Business Model Canvas · Key partners · Value proposition · Customer segments · Revenue · Design thinking

Innovation Starts with Innovation: The Sustainability Lens and the Business Model Canvas

The Business Model Canvas (BMC), developed by Alexander Osterwalder in 2004 as a doctoral dissertation on business model innovation, revolutionized how people approached and engaged in enterprise development (Osterwalder 2004). Osterwalder, a student at Switzerland's HEC Lausanne, worked with professor Yves Pigneur to bring this model to the world. In a time where countless business strategy and management books are published each year, BMC rose above the rest through its innovative, inclusive, open approach (Osterwalder and Pigneur 2010). The team first caught the world's attention through Osterwalder's blog which shared the ideas developed in his dissertation. In time, management from large multinational corporations such as 3M, Deloitte, and Ericsson

T.L. Stenn, *Social Entrepreneurship as Sustainable Development*,
DOI 10.1007/978-3-319-48060-2_4

began using Osterwalder's BMC approach (Businessmodelalchemist 2016). They found BMC to be very effective in building conversations, creating a shared language, supporting brainstorming, team building, collaboration, and creating a structure upon which to implement new ideas and innovations.

Soon blog followers began asking Osterwalder for a book. Rather than contact a publisher and write the book himself, a slow and costly proposal, Osterwalder, decided to crowdsource both the development of the book content and its publishing. He created an online Hub funded through memberships which ranged from $24 to $243 and set out to coauthor the book. In all, 470 practitioners from 45 countries signed up to create the "Business Model Generation" released in 2009. By 2014, over a million copies had been sold (Osterwalder and Pigneur 2010). During the book development, the graphic template known as the BMC was also created and shared globally through the Creative Commons (CC). Founded in 2001 through Duke University's Center for the Study of the Public Domain, CC is a California-based non-profit which supports work in open education, open data, public policy, research, arts and culture, and technology and legal tools (Creativecommons 2016). By 2009, there were over 350 million CC-licensed works for public use including the BMC (Businessmodelgeneration 2016). As of 2014, over 5 million copies of the BMC had been downloaded (Businessmodelgeneration 2016).

Osterwalder believes in making strategy, innovation, and entrepreneurship simple, practical, and applicable (Alexosterwalder 2016). Before BMC, enterprise development was done via long, tedious business plans, reports, and documentation which hindered innovation and made development cumbersome, incomprehensible, and prohibitive, especially in multicultural, multilingual, and even illiterate environments. Much of today's revolutionary growth in innovation and entrepreneurship can be directly traced to BMC's universal appeal and agility in creating a shared global language and intuitive visual mapping. Today BMC is used in classrooms, boardrooms, and community centers across the globe. The book, *Business Model Generation*, has been translated into over 30 different languages and used in more than 250 universities (Businessmodelgeneration 2016).

The BMC is divided into nine sections and can be looked at as a brain map. The right side is comprised of the creative functions: customer segments, customer relationships, access channel value propositions. The left is logistics: key partners, key activities, key resources, and (again) value propositions. The base is made up of revenue—money going out (costs) and coming in (revenue). The model is created to help individuals and groups develop strategies, plans, and make decisions around the different elements of a business. Applying the four quadrants of the sustainability lens (SL) to each of these nine sections of the BMC identified 36 ways in which sustainability can be built. These are not checkpoints, steps, or suggestions but rather ways of thinking and being that collectively enable one to create a more sustainable business and future for the world. All 36 ways do not need to be defined and implemented at once. For example, if in the spirit of design thinking, a conversation is taking place around new product development with the resources and activities parts of the BMC being used and new customer segments researched, one like a detective can hold the SL up to each section to see how the solutions can be directed toward meeting business objectives while also growing sustainability. As businesses get better versed and more adept at using the SL, this becomes more of an intuitive integrated process, rather than an extra layer being added on.

This section will introduce the nine sections of the BMC and show what happens when the SL is held over each, creating new ways in which to effectively realize and manage growth, change, and promote innovation. These sections can be approached in any manner from a logistics perspective to a needs-based perspective. For example, one might have an innovative product in mind and be curious about whom to offer it to or one might see a need and be curious about how a product can fill that need. The canvas can be approached from any starting block. The main blocks are key partners, value proposition, and customer segments. Where one is in the business process would dictate where one would begin. For example, if someone is thinking of starting a company for the first time, they could begin by looking at where there are allies and supports for the endeavor and begin with key partners. Or if a company has a product they already have developed or are passionate about developing and want to know how it can best perform in the market, they can start at value proposition to begin understanding the product more. If someone is identifying a customer need and brainstorming how a product can be developed to meet that need, then they could be starting with the customer segment, exploring the customer more deeply to develop a product that most closely aligns with their needs. Whatever the starting point and wherever one is in the product or company life cycle: early start-up, emerging growth mode, or slowing down in a mature market—the BMC is the map where greater sustainability is discovered using the SL.

Using the BMC

The BMC is a roadmap for all businesses. Already established companies can pick up their SL and begin exploring a product or service from any place on the map. Some companies start at a micro-place of weakness. Perhaps a product is costing a bit more than the market wants and sales are down. Starting with the SL in cost structure can help new ways for product pricing to be imagined. Moving out from there can help to better align the entire organization with a more sustainable perspective.

Others use the SL as a "tune-up" tool where they move it over the BMC road map in a more general, macro enterprise way, looking at their entire organization and seeking clues on how they can improve operations to be more sustainable, strengthen customer relations, and establish a firm place in the market.

To use the BMC for a pre-start-up, as a way to try out an idea or hunch, it is best to begin with key partners as opposed to customer segments, which is where most people may think to start. Key partners help to ground the idea into the reality of possibility. It gives pre-start-ups place to begin and identifies readily available resources. Working from this place gets the initial idea started and is a place to develop a "proof of concept" a way of prototyping, testing, and showing that "yes, this is an available idea that has merit," and that you are the person to work on it. Later pivots can take place, which means that the initial idea still holds but other changes can be made such as additional products added, the customer segment expanded, and more diversity and sustainability taking place.

I find starting with key partners quickly takes one out of the theoretical realm and into the doing mode enabling one to try on the "entrepreneur hat" and see how it fits. Soft skills such as project management, communications, and networking become important. One may realize through this process that running a start-up is not something they enjoy doing, that the idea is more complex than thought, that they are not ready to commit the time and energy needed to see the project through, or that they need partners. These are all important lessons and experiences that starting with key partners quickly pull one into. Many great ideas lose their greatness as they move through the Canvas and key partners helps this to happen in a real time, vivid way. This is an important part of the process of entrepreneurship and does not equate to failure but to invaluable learning and discovery. If an initial idea does sputter out before it becomes a full-fledged enterprise, it can become the fuel for a new approach, a reformation of the team, or an ember to spark a new interest from others.

Using the BMC for Pre-Start-Ups

The following are the recommended steps for a pre-start-up to follow when exploring the BMC with (or without) the SL:

- Key partners: Who is going to help you? What assets do you have? What do you need?
- Value proposition: What are you going to create? Where is that need?
- Customer segments: Who will be using this and how?

And then the logistics...

- Key activities: How will it be made?
- Key resources: By whom and with what?

And the financials:

- Cost structure: How much does it cost? How will you pay for it? Are you sure? Run the numbers and give hearty markups for marketing, distribution, and customer service.
- Revenue streams: Who is going to pay for it? How? When? Where? How often?

And finally the marketing...

- Channels: How will the customer know about it? Get it?
- Customer relationships:... and get it again? How will they tell their friends?

Introduction to Design Thinking

The SL is part of a larger body of thought called design thinking. Design thinking is an interactive, nonlinear, visual way of looking at how things connect. Often used in mapping it consists of seeing patterns and relationships that overlap. The SL is a design-thinking tool. It can be used to look at systems and see new and different ways in which they can connect and transform. The BMC is also a design-thinking tool developed to create more access to business thinking, planning, strategizing, and problem solving. The BMC and SL work together to bring into focus complex relationships and possibilities for building more sustainability within a business. The SL can be used to tightly hone in on a business dynamic such as customer development and go deeply into building more sustainability there.

Gazing through the lens is like looking through a magnifying glass; there will be fuzzy perimeters at first but as the lens is lowered and more tightly focuses, specific ideas begin to take on a sharper form and new details emerge. There will be fuzzy perimeters and mirrored solutions as the effects of one's actions in one area impact how things are realized in others. While the lens will be introduced in the next section in a linear, segment by segment way, it is easier to understand for organizational purposes that it is a much more dynamic tool than that. The dynamism creates redundancy, which is a good thing. Redundancy shows how systems can reinforce each other and strengthen more than one aspect of a business simultaneously. Redundancy also shows where there are dependencies and how one action can impact others in similar ways, amplifying impact.

In theories of design thinking, impact is seen as levers. Levers have a cause/effect relationship. As a lever is turned on or off, it results in different reactions—for example, the growth or constraint of something. Unlike linear models of business development, design thinking is project based and has rules and constraints that direct it. It uses abductive logic, which means the logic of what might be and is open to imagined possibilities. This is very different from deductive and inductive logic which is the logic of what should be or what is and examines proven concepts and known ideas (Dunne and Martin 2006). Abductive logic creates more space for innovation, creativity, and risk. Risk in this case is not negative or reckless, but it is necessary as new ideas are tried (Dunne and Martin 2006). Without risk, there is no innovation.

Innovation by its very nature is a risky business that requires an attempt to know the unknown. Accepting this fact and having a strategy in place to mitigate risk is critical to being a successful innovator. The SL can help develop this strategy and the BMC provides the framework in which to explore it. There are five basic rules when managing innovation, which include working within existing models such as the BMC or other "mental models" that contain the steps and processes necessary to support innovation, knowing that innovation has limitations, expecting and being comfortable with unknowns, and really get the know the person the innovation is for (ERM 2013).

Creating a risk-supportive environment where failure is embraced and celebrated is important for the SL. Failure shows that assumptions are being stretched and new ideas are forming around each other. In a risk-supportive environment, future events and possibilities are seen in a non-judgmental cause and effect manner enabling new thought models to develop (Dunne and Martin 2006). Thinking is also collaborative and interactive. The SL is a team tool for use in group discussions, workshops, and retreats that encourage participants to challenge current practices and assumptions, seek out alternatives and engage in new approaches. It is a dynamic, design-thinking tool that creates positive change.

Design thinking is about visualizing and imagining something that does not currently exist and would take care of users' needs. It is about prototyping, giving the product to the consumer and then improving it. In today's business terms, this is called the pivot and is based on the Lean Startup way of thinking (Ries 2011). The Lean Startup is a three-tier pyramid. On the first tier, the base, an idea is grounded in a single solid idea or vision (Ries 2011). This is pretty solid and rarely moves or changes. For example, KUSIKUY, my company, is an alpaca knitwear company; that aspect will never change. The next tier is a slightly more flexible strategy, or plan. This is devised around the vision to bring it to fruition and is changeable but in a slower way (Ries 2011). In the KUSIKUY example, the vision could be the production model of the women hand-knitting at home, a cottage industry approach. The strategy could change if we decided to use handknitting looms in a central location that the women traveled to. We would still have the vision of creating alpaca clothing, but the strategy shifted. The third tier, the top of the pyramid, is the product or service which is always being optimized and improved in a fast-paced, continuous way; often without a lot of data, but in a quick "let's see what happens" manner. Social media and targeted online approaches support this approach. In the KUSIKUY example, products could be the size, style, and color of the garments produced. The product and the strategy are the pivots, places where change can happen while the vision stays grounded and immobile. This is how businesses and products can change rapidly and strategically, being more agile (Ries 2011). The SL works in the environment of the pivot and design thinking—giving permission for different approaches to be identified, adapted, and implemented without changing the core essence of the company.

The SL and Key Partnerships

Key partnerships are of particular importance for businesses. These are the people and organizations that make new projects possible by providing space, expertise, and/or infrastructure. Some may have a direct financial interest in one's work. Others may have surplus resources to share or mutual interests. By forming partnerships, businesses can gain access to resources and reduce risk. The BMC identified four different types of partnerships: strategic alliance between both noncompetitions and competitors, joint ventures for new businesses and buyer–supplier relationships. Partnerships can result in a shared office or warehousing space, shared shipping services, bulk purchasing of goods, research, or a guaranteed market for waste. Even for established businesses, revisiting key partnerships, especially with the SL, creates new ways in which organizations can work together and tie in with different resources.

The SL helps to illuminate even more possibilities in this area. For example, looking at key partnerships and resources brings about active engagement for collaboration in energy production, supply chain management, waste management, and research. The drive for knowledge and diversity creates many new and creative ways to approach this. It is not a passive response but one that supports innovation and shared risk with the end goal of continually developing the most sustainable solutions possible.

Case Study—New Belgium Beer Company

An example of how a social enterprise's practices could be understood from an SL perspective is as follows. In 2007, Colorado-based New Belgium Beer Company partnered with the City of Fort Collins, Colorado State University and other energy-focused companies to apply for a grant from the Department of Energy to demonstrate how they could help support a 20–30 % peak electric load reduction (New Belgium 2016). New Belgium along with private investors helped fund a $3 million system at the brewery to create 1000 kW of electricity through solar PV, cogeneration, metering, and controls (New Belgium 2016).

By focusing on the SL resources and key partners to actively seek new solutions, radically new approaches to energy production and waste management can emerge. At New Belgium, for example, this included composting waste (mash) into biofuel, and building relationships with new partners—a university, federal and local government, and private individuals. By focusing on the SL health and key partners something different emerges; the growth of trust and relationships with sources outside of the company itself. A deep connection to the community emerges through this project as it grows opportunities and capabilities through innovation. By focusing on the SL policy and key partners the inclusion of government and the community in finding and funding mutually beneficial solutions is key. By focusing on the SL exchange and key partners New Belgium achieved more through working with others than they ever would have on their own. The cost of the entire project was over $11 million of which Belgium Brewing personally committed $1.5 million for an energy system that directly supported their operation; 60 % of the project funding came from government grants while the remainder was paid by private industry and public investors. By intentionally using the SL to actively seek new ways in which to find and engage with key partners, New Belgium is now no longer just another business in the community—or even just another brewery, but instead is deeply linked as a key leader in building a more sustainable and healthy community (New Belgium 2016).

The SL + key resources = actively seek mutually beneficial partnerships from many diverse places (key resources can be physical, financial, intellectual, or human)

The SL and Value Propositions

Also known as the "Unique Selling Point", the value proposition is the bundled benefits or features that a product or service brings that are different from all others. This can be realized in the product or services' function, form (delivery), production, or story and can be a combination of elements. It may be innovative and represent a new or disruptive offer; one that challenges industry or societal norms such as a clothing company that makes affordable fashions without sweatshop labor, environmental, or human rights abuses. In this sense, social entrepreneurships (SEs) can be considered industry disrupters. Or it can be performance based, being better than other products or services in its class or perhaps customized to uniquely address a very specific need. What makes the value proposition so important is its appeal to a specific client need or problem; it is very closely aligned to and able to change with the customer segments. The SL illuminates, even more, possibilities for customer connections in this area.

When applying the SL to value proposition (SL value proposition), a myriad of possibilities arise. Here through products or services offered emerges new opportunities to source and use materials differently, build unique customer relations, emerge as a community advocate and change maker, and participate in a diversified economy. Building advocacy is key in generating long-lasting results, customer loyalty, and influence sustainability for others.

Looking through the resources segment of the SL (SL resources), there arise opportunities for educating customers on an organization's innovative solutions. These can address common customer values such as the need for sustainable energy, production that has a low environmental impact, the use of natural ingredients, low energy inputs, and sourcing ethical products or services.

SL health illuminates the customer's desire to understand how a product or service helps others but also their need for community, celebration, and love. Today's customers are seeking a place of belonging, a shared spirit of camaraderie, and a way to connect more deeply with others. In addition, health is about being inclusive and reaching out to marginalized people and disadvantaged populations to create and build opportunity for them. It could be manifested, for example, by purchasing only from women, or purposely hiring people who have been previously incarcerated or intentionally making a workplace friendly for transgendered youth. The important thing is that an organization is purposely looking to add value to the product by growing sustainability through the betterment of the health and well-being of the community.

Moving to policy in the SL (SL policy) creates opportunities for companies to take on the role of a change agent and inspire and engage customers in it as well. Policy takes one out of the passive role of doing good for oneself or one's organization and becomes an example of how doing good can work for others too. This is not creating competition—rather it is creating admiration. By making one's company an example of something done really well, others become inspired and empowered to strive to be better too. Growing sustainability for one's business enables them to become a rising star for the world community.

When applying the SL to exchange (SL exchange) one is looking at more creative ways in which customers can engage in product, whether through wholesale or bulk buying, shares that one can own in the company, memberships, working credits, or volunteer activities. SL exchange is also about minimizing inequality, a leading challenge in sustainability. Exchanges can be made more equal through the disbursement of earnings in creative ways that do not lead to feelings of loss but instead strengthen the business and the community. For example, a business can disburse surplus through donations, sponsorships, and community service.

Case Study—Sundial Brands

An example of how SL policy works with a value proposition can be seen in a case study of Richelieu Dennis of Sundial Brands. Dennis engaged in what would be SL policy with a value proposition when he used his experience producing products that cater to ethnic skin needs and stores' positioning of his products to highlight racial inequalities in how stores portray beauty (Sundial 2016). He launched a social media campaign #BreakTheWalls bringing attention to the fact that Sundial beauty brands were sold as "ethnic" in leading chain stores, separate from the traditional beauty sections (Segran 2016). His campaign challenged, "Is ethnic not beautiful?" and "Am I not beautiful?" highlighting the shopping experience from an African American woman's perspective as she passes by the beauty section of the store to find her own products sold separately, not as beauty but as "ethnic" (Segran 2016).

Sundial Brands is a US-based, Fair Trade natural beauty product line favored by millions of black consumers. The campaign went viral bringing in 300 million impressions on social media (Segran 2016). It did not target selling product, but brought attention to larger issues of perception, equality, and inclusion, gaining more users including ones outside the black community and Sundial brand's current customer base. As a result of this campaign, gross annual sales grew by 31 % to over $200 million in 2015 (Segran 2016).

Note of caution: Using the SL is a holistic exercise. It is not just a tool to prop up a single aspect of an organization or narrowly appeal to a customer segment's specific need, but rather a way in which to reimagine an organization and make it into something that is stronger, more fun, inclusive, proactive, and sustainable, setting an example for others. As the SL applied to value propositions helps companies rise in the public eye through the promotion of their efforts and innovations, it would be expected that these innovations are part of a larger integrated commitment to seeking and growing sustainability. For example, Dennis' Sundial Brands went viral with a social media campaign calling attention to the negative shopping experience that ethnic customers experienced when purchasing his product. However, Sundial Brands also had a product that was made of organic, natural materials, was Fair Trade, and created important jobs for over 2500 women living in Ghana and Turkey. In addition, Sundial Brands has a community commerce team that looks for ways Sundial can give back to local community, for example, donating 10 % of gross sales of community commerce products back into local initiatives. This full circle approach that Dennis takes with his company from employing women, reaching out to the underprivileged, protecting the environment by using only natural ingredients, giving back to the community and making meaningful social change—collectively is what helped this company to grow and be so successful, not just the #BreakTheWalls campaign. It is important to remember that when using the SL, it is often exciting and easy to find compelling value propositions to focus on, but without taking a deeper look at other aspects of one's product or services, such as production, energy use, environmental and human impact, and all of the segments in the BMC, the value proposition could be seen by others as "greenwashing." Greenwashing is when an insincere social message is created solely to generate sales or positive publicity without any deep thought or commitment being made. This feeling of insincerity can create a negative campaign rather than a positive one as greenwashing is often associated with in-authenticity, deceit, and untrustworthiness.

Best Practices Value Propositions and the SL

There is an interesting correlation between the six best practices of high-impact nonprofits as identified in the book *Forces for Good* by authors Leslie Crutchfield and Heather McLeod Grant and value propositions as viewed from the SL (2012). High-impact nonprofits were defined as ones that built social movements and were innovators in their fields; transforming business, government, other nonprofits, and individuals in their practices and thinking; and changed the world around them (Crutchfield and McLeod Grant 2012). High-impact nonprofits also had the basics needed to sustain their impact they attracted and retained good talent, found sustainable sources of funding, and invested into their infrastructure and capacity.

Crutchfield and McLeod Grant spent several years following 12 high-impact nonprofit organizations identified via a national peer survey of 2790 executive directors of nonprofits to discover what practices they used which made them so successful (Crutchfield and McLeod Grant 2012). After studying public information, visiting the organizations, conducting interviews with founders and leaders, and analyzing budget data, compensation rates, turnover rates, and organizational charts, patterns began to emerge. The six best practices of high-impact nonprofit organizations were to

1. work with government and advocate for policy change;
2. harness market forces and see business as a powerful partner;
3. convert individual supporters into evangelists for the cause;
4. build and nurture nonprofit networks, treating other groups as allies;
5. adapt to the changing environment; and
6. share leadership, empowering others to be forces for good (forcesforgood.net, 2016).

What is interesting about these findings is that that they are very similar to the approaches illuminated by SL value proposition and the way it intersects with how the product or service is of importance to the consumer and how the consumer wants to share this importance with others. For example, businesses and consumers both can become inspired to become an advocate and create a community of support for the practices followed and promoted by the organization enabling others to take charge—sharing and growing leadership.

The SL + value proposition = be the example by building advocacy and community around the work you do creating new ways for customers to engage in and access product and services.

The SL and Customer Segments

The customer is the heart of every business model. Without the customer, there is no business. This segment changes for every customer and provides a very specific micro view of a unique demographic of customer influenced by age, gender, socioeconomic background, place, employment, ability, culture, behavior, and needs. Often there are multiple customer segments for a single product or service. The key to having a good marketing strategy is to really get to know and understand micro customer segments, building a strong, sustainable customer relationship specifically crafted for your targeted customer segment. To define a customer segment think about the specific type of product or service they need how they will access it, what the long-term relationship will be, and what their profitability is.

From a sustainability perspective, profitability is understood more broadly than just monetary terms. One can look at customer profitability in its strength in motivating others and build a critical mass of support for a new product or service and also as a subsidized space, where some customers may be covering the cost of participation of others thereby creating greater access and diversity for an organization. Viewing the customer segment through the SL brings into focus many new possibilities for building long-lasting, meaningful customer relationships.

Customer segments and SL resources bring into focus ways in which one can help customers to be more educated and mindful of their own use of resources. While the enterprise itself is becoming more resourceful in its product development and services, it can empower customers with tools and education so they can do the same, presenting new ways in which customers can better understand their own supply chains when sourcing goods and services for their own needs. This empowers consumers helping them to take roles as advocates and collective change makers.

Sustainability is an interrelated concept that like a pebble thrown into a still lake has rippling effects that impact all around it. Resources in the SL is about active learning and the mindful use of energy, water, air, and habitat; the generation of energy; mitigation of waste; and sharing of knowledge to enable others to make informed decisions. When an enterprise introduces the concept of identifying raw materials, energy inputs, and a sustainable supply chain created and management by customers and then offers products or services as models of how this can work, strong relationships, trust, community, and advocacy are built. In this way, businesses also empower customers to further develop and seek more sustainable supply chains for themselves, their own communities and regions, laying the path to a larger movement of overall sustainability. These communities, in turn, can educate the larger public and take action leading to better policy. This relationship and sequence will be examined more as one moves through the quadrants of the SL.

Looking at customer segments with SL health creates ways in which relationships can be built focusing on family, love, recreation, belief, memory, and meaning. This is where histories can be developed, timelines made, legends and founder stories told, milestones set, and generations built. The evolution of the enterprise and the growth of the people within it are important. Milestones can be celebrated as well as anniversaries. Creating a place where customers share experiences and ideas openly with each other is important here too. Building the health segment of the SL can do on the local level through community potlucks where guests bring food or projects share; open monthly, quarterly, or annual meetings that can be attended in person but also via teleconferencing and social media; and open house tours of the facility. Parties and celebrations are an important part of health. Talent shows, open mike nights, and sharing on social media are also important.

Some other ways in which business grow the SL health particularly for attracting new customers is through educational tours where producers or suppliers are invited to meet with the public and share stories with others. This can be partnered with existing events such as fairs, conferences, trade shows, or retail events. It can also be done through higher-ed institutions or schools via through classroom visits or via social media, podcasts, and video. Live presentations have greater impact than recorded ones though recorded presentations have greater reach. Thinking about who the customer segment is will guide the selection of the right place for an educational tour and outreach. Giving existing and potential customers tools in which they can celebrate their own success and share ideas with each other is another way to grow health. They can be encouraged to show themselves using the product, being innovative with their use, or engaging in the product or service in new, beautiful, or exciting ways. This can be done via a Facebook page, Instagram post, Pinterest board, or other forms of social media.

Customer segments and SL policy create a place for empowered consumers to advocate for change on a broader level branching from their own practices to that of their community, region, country, and world. It takes lessons learned in SL resources and SL health and encourages consumers to bring them to the public for consideration, discussion, and coalition building. Policy is not about radicalization and revolution, rather it is tempered by Ruray which seeks and tolerates differences and when mixed with Circles' policy, encourages dialogue, discussion, and reconciliation. An enterprise can help support this process by creating space for discussion through panel presentations, open idea generation, and community projects that naturally guide customers to a place of creative discourse and collaborative problem solving that engage them with the product or service in a favorable and creative way.

When looking at customer segments and SL exchange again, diversity in the way in which products and information are accessed and used becomes important. Here clubs and affinity groups can develop along with partnerships with others who can support the creation of more opportunities for members and other businesses to engage in greater supply chain, energy, or environmental sustainability.

Case Study—Equal Exchange

The following is an example of how the SL can be used in a customer segment. Equal Exchange is a worker-owned cooperative based out of Boston, Massachusetts, which partners with farmer cooperatives in Latin America. The farmers produce export commodities such as coffee, chocolate, and bananas. Equal Exchange purchases these goods at a fair price and transforms and resells products to US consumers, creating important market access to farmers and well-produced goods to consumers. An example of Equal Exchange's use of the SL in the customer segment can be seen in their "Fair Trade Halloween" and nonprofit organization, Global Exchange's "reverse trick or treating" campaigns (Equal Exchange 2016; Global Exchange 2016). Though having similar names, these two organizations are not related to each other with Equal Exchange being based out of Boston and Global Exchange being in San Francisco. However, both are committed to Fair Trade and justice and both have campaigns are aimed at educating the public about the prevalence of child labor in mainstream chocolate and the benefits that Equal Exchange's chocolate, made without child labor, brings to producer families.

Traditionally in the United States, trick or treating happens on or around October 31st in celebration of Halloween and is about children dressing up in costumes and visiting homes in their neighborhood to receive free candy from private households. In 2015, US consumers spent $2.5 billion on Halloween candy according to the National Confectioners Association (NCA) (NCA 2014). Unfortunately, most of this was sold as inexpensive bags of prepackaged, low-quality Halloween candy filled with sugar, artificial colors, flavors, and inexpensive ingredients. Inexpensive ingredients do not allow much earnings for producers, resulting in the reliance on cheap child labor in chocolate production and enslaved workers on sugar plantations (Haney 2007). Seventy percent of the world's chocolate comes from West Africa where more than 2 million children are enslaved in cocoa production, according to the Tulane University and the US Department of Labor's 7-year study of the region (Tulane University 2015). This is an illegal practice worldwide; however, it is hard to enforce in West Africa where in 2014 there are poor labor laws, corruption, a growing demand for cocoa (the raw materials in chocolate), a growing population and not many opportunities for children (Tulane University 2015). In addition, the US government does not hold candy companies responsible for unfair labor practices in their supply chains. The story of child labor in chocolate, though well documented and easily tracked to companies such as Nestle, Hershey, and Mars, goes largely unreported in most mainstream press, resulting in consumers largely unknowingly purchasing billions of dollars of candy made with child slave labor (O'Keefe 2016).

Equal Exchange as a company is committed to sustainability, workers' rights, environmental protection, and no child labor (Equal Exchange 2016). They are careful to source ethically grown chocolate (Equal Exchange 2016). To increase the quality and value of the chocolate, they offer farmers technical training and access to organic certifications (Equal Exchange 2016). This helps to protect the earth from harmful nonorganic agriculture practices and pesticides and creates more value for the chocolate. The result is a more expensive, higher quality, chocolate product. Studies have found that consumers are willing to pay more for their products if they understand why it costs more and the benefits it brings (Stenn 2013). Studies have also found that it is important to be informed about the negative effect that cheaper products have on people and the planet (Stenn 2013). This is true in the case of chocolate too.

Equal Exchange's "Fair Trade Halloween" consists of an online and event-based model that is highly shareable both on social media and via live presentations and community actions (Equal Exchange 2016). There is a simple, informative 2-min video explaining the shortcomings of non-fair trade chocolate production and the benefits Equal Exchange brings to farmers (Equal Exchange 2016). Plus, there are free, downloadable lessons, activities, fundraisers, flyers, videos, PowerPoint presentations, catalogs, and tools for teachers, clubs, households, and the general public to use to create their own events. There are also examples of others' work, a toll-free 800 number to call for help with organizing an event, success studies, fundraising campaigns, and more ways to take action either through tabling, community education, or consumption—both on an individual scale and an office group environment (Equal Exchange 2016).

The tone of the campaigns is playful and non-vindictive with a theme of "Believe it or not...chocolate can be scary!" coupled with a positive, solutions-based approach (Equal Exchange 2016). Other campaign themes include "Buy Equal Exchange chocolate. Products you can feel good about offering to your community. Make your office a better place. Make a difference in your community" (Equal Exchange 2016). These messages empowered the consumer to take action to educate others, and inadvertently, sell Equal Exchange products.

Global Exchange, a San Francisco-based nonprofit that promotes social, economic justice around the world, echoed Equal Exchange's campaign by launching a complementary Reverse Trick or Treating promotion with similar online tools (Global Exchange 2016). There is a video, printable handouts and a kit that can be purchased and delivered with preprinted cards explaining the concept behind Reverse Trick or Treating, data on the hardships faced by West African children in the coffee industry and small samples of Equal Exchange organic, Fair Trade chocolate (Global Exchange 2016). The campaign goal is to educate consumers by having participants to purchase mini Equal Exchange chocolates, tape them to an information card, and have children hand them back to consumers when trick or treating to inform them of the hardships West African children are facing and to ask that they not support this.

Equal Exchange commented on this approach, "The inspiration for Reverse Trick-or-Treating rests on the belief that the simple act of one person saying to another, 'There's a problem. There's a solution. Let's do something,' can be very powerful. And if a child says this to an adult—it's doubly powerful. Further, we believe that such acts will demonstrate to the large corporations, and to public officials, that people are paying attention, people care, and they want action" (Borden 2014).

Looking at Equal Exchange's "Fair Trade Halloween" and Global Exchange's "reverse trick or treating" through the SL shows how many of the ideas brought into by the lens look when implemented. For example, the SL resources aspect focuses on educating and empowering others on the importance of personal supply chain management while SL health focused on empowerment, community building, and advocacy, which is exactly what each of these campaigns is doing. SL policy looks at how people can talk about new ways of approaching things and both campaigns focus on education and dialogue echo this as well. None are confrontational nor involve negative or cohesive actions such as strikes, boycotts, or horrific photos of enslaved, starving children. Rather there is a feeling of respect and constraint as data is shared on the positive results of the well-sourced, fairly paid chocolate. Images and testimonials show healthy farms and happy families with children well fed and in school. In these campaigns, there is no blame or shame placed on the buyer of the harmful candies, rather dialogues are opened, often for the first time and information shared. Finally, the SL exchange is engaged largely through volunteerism. It is supported by people taking the initiative to find, download, and use the interactive activities: teaching lessons to others and getting clubs, groups, teams, and the workforce involved. It is also about exchanging goods for time. By inviting people to sample the product, supporters are buying a person's attention so more information can be shared and conversations begun. Usually, the samples are purchased by the volunteers themselves to help them to spread the message they feel so passionate about.

The SL + customer segments = creatively empower and engaged current and potential customers to act as ambassadors and advocates for sustainability practices developed by the enterprise.

The SL and Key Resources

Key resources are the inputs needed to create the products or services delivered. These include physical, intellectual, human, and financial assets. Examples of each include the physical building or place of work, machinery, supplies, technology, skills, labor, and capital to run the operation.

Looking at key resources through SL resources, opportunities emerge to actively seek materials that are energy efficient, have a low environmental impact, produce little or no waste, respect workers by providing safe workplaces, fair pay, and supporting people in living the life they have reason to value. This includes built structures—where energy generation, use, and Leadership in Energy and Environmental Design (LEEDS) certification become important, land use and management and following the supply chain of every input all of the way down to its extraction or harvest from the earth.

SL health promotes the formation of close, respectful, relationships with suppliers and contractors. Treating them like family, taking time to socialize outside of work, remembering birthdays and anniversaries, and paying invoices on time are all a part of this special part of sustainability. So is working together collaboratively with transparency, honesty, respect, and striving for win-win solutions that benefit both parties.

SL policy and key resources are open and honest ways to build contacts, source product, make hiring decisions, support the workforce through adequate paid vacations, time for volunteerism, personal time off, and flex time. It is about creating a safe space for open conversation, dialogue, and input from all about the best practices for the organization. It also includes a democratized workplace that gives others the power to make this happen.

Exchange is seen as giving back through volunteerism, a percentage of earnings put into a community development fund, events, donations, and sponsorships. Barter, the trading of goods for goods rather than currency, is also a way of exchange as is time trade, the trading goods for time, and the use or development of local currencies—regional money circulated within a specific place. Making an effort to source products locally when possible and creating ways for small suppliers or new start-ups to be involved with a larger firm is also important here. Specific ways that a larger company can help smaller suppliers or new start-ups to grow is to be a mentor to that company, introduce that company to other potential customers, provide a testimonial for the company and inclusion in social media, place orders that align with the company's current capacity with a commitment to purchase more when capacity grows, pre-pay orders, share discounts when ordering in bulk, and in general take a proactive, benevolent interest in the organization.

The SL + key resources = seek new, creative ways to source local, ethically made materials while also looking for opportunities to help invest in or grow others social enterprises.

Key Activities

Key activities are the things that need to happen in order for the product or service to be ready for the customer. This is largely a human resources function with management, leadership, communications, and logistical demands. It also includes accounting, manufacturing, problem solving, research, and development. The key activities are the most important actions a company needs to take in order to operate successfully.

In SL resources, key activities empower organizations to develop the core sustainability elements they have been seeking from others in key resources, where supply chains are scrutinized for being energy efficient, having a low environmental impact, producing little or no waste, respecting the workers by providing safe workplaces and enabling people to live a life they have reason to value. Here in key activities, organizations are able to be innovative and actively seek out better solutions for waste management and transformation; resource usage and reusage; energy creation and reduction, controlling one's own environmental footprint and setting an example for others. Here key partners can play an important role by assisting in the research and development of new approaches, partnering in joint ventures or shared systems, and providing financial, intellectual, and human capital.

The SL health enables an organization to create the best workplace ever. Here employees can be empowered through voting and participation in decisions, learning and development opportunities, skills building, job sharing, and creating synergy by working together in well-managed teams—sharing wins and milestones. Health also supports flexibility in the workday, scheduling and timing and creates a balance for workers so there is time for family and friendships along with steady work. Having access to good health care is also an important part of this as is having a safe and healthy work environment to work in with means for advancement and meaningful work.

SL policy is seen in participation. This means creating opportunities for dialogues to form around key activities and their impacts both internally in the workforce and organization and externally within the community and natural environment. This encourages the development of public forums and workshops to educate people about activities, learn about their impacts and enable others to express views and concerns, engage in dialogues, seek and embrace a diversity of ideas, keeping in mind the Andean model where all is different and neither good or bad, nor right or wrong and opposites are needed to make up a whole. Sustainability demands that one seeks out opposites, listens, and lets new, collaborative ways to approach things emerge.

SL exchange creates an internal version of SL exchange in key resources. Here volunteerism, barter, time trade, and local currencies can be used within the organization to build more camaraderie, solidarity, and help diversify the way in which resources are acquired and shared and work is done. This can be as simple as having a "grab bag" of extra office supplies for people to use at work or at home, desk shares or mobile office space, shared potluck lunches where people prepare dishes to share with each other, on-site day care for children and pets staffed by worker volunteers who get credit for time spent with their own children and pets, and profit sharing in organizational earnings.

The SL + key resources + key activities = build an inclusive, democratic, empowered workforce with flexible scheduling open forums and a healthy work environment.

Case Study—Fair Trade

Largely viewed as a way of bringing social justice to the world's most impoverished, Fair Trade is participatory model that relies on institutions to help businesses promote economic justice and build freedom through cooperation and solidarity between producers and buyers. It focuses on cultural diversity, gender equality, environmental sustainability, long-term development, and greater economic return with specific guidelines to direct this. FINE stands for four international Fair Trade institutions: FLO; IFAT [now the World Fair Trade Federation (WFTO)]; Network of European World Shops (NEWS), a consortium of Fair Trade retail outlets; and the European Fair Trade Association (EFTA) which serves Fair Trade importers (Stenn 2013). FINE describes Fair Trade's mission in the following way:

> Fair trade is a trading partnership, based on dialogue, transparency, and respect, that seeks greater equity in international trade. It contributes to sustainable development by offering better trading conditions to, and securing the rights of, marginalized producers and workers—especially in the South. Fair trade organizations, backed by consumers, are engaged actively in supporting producers, awareness raising and in campaigning for changes in the rules and practice of conventional international trade. (2006)

This mission is upheld by different guidelines, known as standards. These standards are closely aligned with ones seen when exploring key activities and key resources through the SL. The Fair Trade standards and their corresponding SL quadrants (presented in parentheses) are listed here:

- Standard One: Creating opportunities for economically disadvantaged producers. (SL health)
- Standard Two: Providing transparency and accountability in management and commercial relations. (SL policy)
- Standard Three: Engaging in trading practices that show a concern for the social, economic, and environmental well-being of producers and do not maximize profit at their expense. (SL health)
- Standard Four: Paying a fair price to producers. (SL exchange)
- Standard Five: Refraining from using child or forced labor in production. (SL health)
- Standard Six: Promoting nondiscrimination, gender equity, and the freedom to organize among producers. (SL health)
- Standard Seven: Providing a safe and healthy working environment. (SL resources)
- Standard Eight: Building capacity by providing opportunities for positive developmental among small, marginalized producers. (SL health)

- Standard Nine: Promoting Fair Trade by raising awareness of the aim of Fair Trade and the need for greater justice in world trade through Fair Trade. (SL policy)
- Standard Ten: Protecting the environment through the production of products which maximize the use of raw materials from sustainably managed, local (when possible) sources (SL resources) (standards sourced from WFTO 2012).

In addition to standards, many certified Fair Trade programs also have community investment funds where a percentage of sales is set aside for community projects such as building schools, roads, and improving community infrastructure enabling Fair Trade to provide services that local governments often cannot. This is similar to SL outcomes from key activities.

It is interesting to note that the Fair Trade guidelines focus heavily on the health aspect of the SL with 50 % of the standards being located in this area. This is reflected in how Fair Trade is understood by the general public with many people identifying Fair Trade as something that helps disadvantaged people (Stenn 2013). However, sustainability is not just about people, it is also about resources, energy, education, engagement, and access. Continuing to look at the Fair Trade standards through the SL, resources, and policy each make up 20 % of the standards while exchange only accounts for 10 %. This imbalance can affect the overall sustainability of Fair Trade and shows a potential weakness. In Fair Trade, consumer access can be hindered by higher prices, perceived or real, and a feeling of exclusiveness. For example, economically disadvantaged people in the United States comment on how they cannot afford Fair Trade or state sarcastically that they need some fair trade for themselves (Stenn 2013). This feeling of disempowerment or association of Fair Trade purchasing with high costs is a challenge for the industry. Using the SL exchange to build more access to Fair Trade in key resources and key activities can strengthen Fair Trade as an institution.

Taking a broader view, fairness and justice are parts of both Fair Trade and sustainability so it is not surprising to find Fair Trade practices easily embedded within an SL framework. To clarify, Fair Trade as an institution can use the entire BC and SL for its own internal assessment, however, as a resource to its subscribers, Fair Trade in this example was examined as a key resource and key activity. One can also view Fair Trade as an SL value proposition for clients.

The SL and Cost Structures and Revenue Streams

Cost structures and revenue streams together make up the base of an organization and need to be strong and deep in order to hold it up. Cost structures look at the financial inputs or investments needed to create a product or service and the revenue stream is about the outputs or earnings that the service or product will generate. The reason why costs and revenue are looked at now and not sooner in this model is to give one a chance to dream and think about a sustainable enterprise without being hindered by concerns about costs. However, costs (and revenue) are core elements of any enterprise and need careful consideration. Viewing cost structures and revenue streams from the perspective of the SL creates new possibilities and grows opportunities.

Cost Structure

The cost structure describes all costs incurred to operate a business. These include costs associated with key partners (innovation), value propositions (marketing), customer segments (sales), and key resources and activities (production). A budget organization is cost driven, competing for markets based on minimizing costs wherever possible while a luxury organization can be value driven looking to deliver premium goods or services with a personalized, exclusive focus. Enterprises fall between the two extremes of budget versus luxury on the cost structures scale. Cost structure includes fixed and variable costs as well as economies of scale and scope. When considering budgets it is advisable to have the best case, worse case, and probable scenarios to measure. This helps one to anticipate the social, environmental, and organizational impact that growth (scale) will bring to an enterprise and the minimum amount of revenue needed for viability. From a sustainability perspective, viewing cost structure with constraint is important because contrary to popular business beliefs, unlimited or too rapid growth is not always a positive or sustainable outcome.

Looking at SL resources and cost structure highlights the types of financial institutions one chooses to partner with. Similar to the way one scrutinizes the supply chain by sourcing supplies all the way down to the most basic raw materials, following them to where they are originally extracted from the earth, the SL resources do the same but with capital. Resources drive one to actively research and seek financial institutions which bring the greatest benefit to people and the planet. This makes small Savings and Loans (S&L) banks preferable over large investment banks because earnings are more tied to local community and are more accessible for neighbors. In addition, cooperative banks also become favorable because of the shared resources they bring and the democratized access to capital, as all depositors are also members. Larger businesses often have investment funds. How these funds are managed becomes important too since investments into unsustainable activities, though sometimes lucrative at first, ultimately affect overall sustainability in a negative way. Fortunately, there are emerging many new social investment options.

Looking at cost structure and SL health through the SL also brings in SL exchange by creating options for others in helping with deciding the type of financial institution to work with. The solution may be the use of both a monetary S&L and nonmonetary Time Bank for an organization—appealing to both social and financial needs in multiple ways. Another equally creative solution may arise as health and exchange complement each other. Viewed together, many new options arise enabling one to grow greater diversity when addressing the costs of production.

SL policy enables organizations to think anew about how resources for production will be accessed. Perhaps there is a shared use, shared workspace, rent to own, or community tool bank options that can help an organization share the financial burden of having access to resources.

Revenue Streams

The revenue stream focuses on how a product or service is paid for. This is where real value is built and earnings emerge. There are many different pricing mechanisms for revenue streams such as fixed pricing, wholesale or volume pricing, auctioned pricing, and market or yield-dependent pricing. There are also different ways in which revenue can be generated either through individual one-time sales (direct ownership), longer term, multiple time/volume contracts, and/or regularly recurring revenue sources such as subscriptions, memberships, or rentals. Some businesses can have a mix of revenue stream options, for example, offering product as a direct buy but also having a rental option.

Businesses do not have a tremendous amount of influence when looking at revenue streams and SL resources. SL resources are about seeking the best sources for energy, materials, and production while minimizing impacts on ecosystems and maximizing social benefits. Since this interaction is largely initiated by the consumer themselves, there is not much place for a company to exert influence. Looking at SL health, a relationship could be made with a lending institution, bank, or credit card that has a social or local benefit associated with it. Though the customer themselves will be ones using this style of socially responsible credit, the business can take an active role by educating and encouraging people to use more socially responsible forms of payment by creating bonuses or incentives with purchases.

When looking at revenue streams and SL health more action can be taken to form long-term relationships with customers, provide ongoing service and support, and give the customer a place to make decisions. This will be addressed in more detail in customer relationships. Revenue streams and policy as seen through the SL is about terms and agreements with a preference for community involvement and dialogue. More about SL policy will be seen in customer relations.

SL exchange is specifically about how the product or service is paid for. Actively seeking diverse ways of exchange grows opportunities, inclusion, and diversity among customers, minimizing risk, and growing one's customer base. There are many creative options for exchange found in the ideas of social solidarity economy. Some options include a "pay as you can" or sliding scale program where customers choose their own price for a product, flexible payment terms with low interest or no interest lending for a period of time, product sharing where multiple people purchase and use a product or service together, monthly memberships, buying clubs for bulk discounts, and gifting clubs which enable others to give products to others—building accessibility. Another SL exchange solution is the creation of scholarships to create more access for others who are not as well off or hybrid models that accept work or barter in addition to or instead of currency for a good or service.

The SL + cost structure + revenue streams = diversify financials by acquiring and disbursing materials and goods beyond the use of a singular currency.

Case Study—Lentil as Anything

Lentil as Anything, a nonprofit Australian restaurant chain with four locations serving over a million meals a year, is an example of how the SL can be used in several creative ways. Since 2000, Lentil as Anything, founded by Shanaka Fernando, has prepared hot breakfasts, lunches, and dinners daily using fresh, local ingredients some of which are donated a mix of volunteer and paid labor, and a “pay what you feel” revenue model (Worrall 2015). This means that meals are offered with no price, patrons choose to pay what they wish for what they eat. The organization explains they have a “unique financial model that is centered on the values of trust, generosity, and respect that gives people the opportunity to eat out and be social” (Lentil as Anything 2016). Pay as you feel is an example of SL exchange where alternative methods of access are created for the product. It is also an example of SL health where there is value placed on the well-being of others and the trust of others, and the meals are served in an upscale, sit-down style, carefully prepared, and presented by wait staff. “Magic Boxes” are scattered about the restaurants to collect payments.

The cost of preparing and serving a single meal is about $12 per person (Worrall 2015). Total operations costs for Lentil as Anything including salaries, ingredients, rent, and utilities are about $24,000 a week (Worrall 2015). When hundreds of local festival goers crashed the Melbourne branch in 2015, leaving behind a $4,000 tab, Fernando did not sway in his belief in people’s generosity and continued with the pay as you feel model. “We are trying to put the onus on people to show that people are intelligent and people have got integrity,” he explained (Worrall 2015).

In the spirit of SL health, Lentil as Anything is active in education programs—offering internships to student and community projects which they participate in and encourage others to as well. They also support local arts by hosting monthly gallery exhibits and live music at their locations. Valuing multiculturalism and inclusion, also part of SL health, features prominently in Lentil as Anything’s values and is reflected in their mission:

> Caring for people: Provide a wholesome and nutritious meal where money is not a concern.
>
> Promoting Multiculturalism: Fostering an environment of inclusion and not exclusion.
>
> Reforming Society: Acting on the structures of society to restore justice. (Lentil as Anything 2016)

SL policy is engaged through Lentil as Anything’s mission of “hiring volunteers, the long-term unemployed and the marginalized” and their value of “being an advocate for the disadvantaged” (Lentil as Anything 2016). SL resources are addressed through the practice of purchasing local ingredients, growing their own on donated farmland, as well as outsourcing their merchandise through Society6, an online organization that supports the production of work by artists worldwide.

The results after more than a decade of operations is an economically successful model which has expanded to three locations, improved people's lives, and includes a large community of supporters and advocates. When one of Lentil as Anything's leases was not going to get renewed, the community sprang to their support and made sure the restaurant stayed in its current location. When a large bill was left unpaid, a community member donated her farmland to the restaurant to use for production and everyday patrons pay more than the $12 a meal enabling everyone in their community a chance to enjoy a good meal in a clean, supportive, respectful environment.

The SL and Channels

Channels are the ways in which customer segments gain access to a product or service. Channels can be realized via a partner such as a delivery company, bundled with other goods or services in a department store model or a mixed product online shopping site, on their own as a direct sale from a retail location, or in a mix of these ways. Channels can be direct or indirect. Direct channels are ones that businesses own and maintain themselves usually as a private website, store, or both. These have an initial setup cost plus maintenance. Indirect channels are managed by someone outside of the business and focus on wholesale volume and moving product. In indirect channels, the business customer is the wholesaler though the product customer—the end user—is also important as the product or service being offered must ultimately appeal to them. A business can realize higher profit margins through direct channel sales, rather than through indirect ones, though each sale costs more and takes more work too. For example, a business selling their product via a brick and motor store is accessing a direct channel for reaching their customer segment, and needs to invest time and money into promoting the store and its products, via events, sales, advertising and promotions, customer service, and social media. If that same business were to sell through an indirect channel, their main needs would be to attach wholesale buyers and get finished product to them. Any additional customer contact, in this case, would fall under customer relationships, and not channels.

Whether direct or indirect, channels have five phases: awareness, evaluation, purchase, delivery, and after sales. Together these form a large part of the customer (user) experience (UX) (Osterwalder and Pigneur 2010). Often multiple channels are offered for a single product or service. When properly approached, channels can make the work and thought put into carefully developing sustainable products more visible and tangible, set an example and inspire customers, and build one's customer base and sales and customers share their experiences with others. The most effective sales media is word of mouth. Channels are the place where this can be created.

Viewing channels through SL resources brings into focus the need to actively research and learn about better ways of making product access meaningful, memorable, and inspirational. Specifically, SL resources are looking at the logistics in how products or services are physically delivered and requires an entire supply chain analysis of all people, materials, and energy impacted all the way down to the earth that materials were extracted or grown from. Both emissions from transportation and waste from packaging become significant here. Scrutinizing delivery in such an intense, mindful manner brings into focus many creative ways in which to innovate.

For example, packaging now becomes very important as one examines the materials and processes needed for safe delivery and a memorable, shareable user experience. From an environmental perspective, less packaging is best since fewer resources and energy are being used to create the packaging. However, from a marketing and logistics perspective, packaging is necessary to delight customers, communicate value propositions, and provide product protection. Packaging should be approached with the same scrutiny and care one puts into the development of the product or service and is the customer's first impression of who you are and what you do. SL resources enable one to seek innovative solutions to packaging needs by thinking creatively about what packaging needs to achieve, what can be eliminated or reduced, which materials will be used, and their impact from a value chain perspective. SL resources in channels require one to consider the raw materials, inputs, energy, waste, and labor associated with the packaging. One can look for innovative win-win solutions in SL resources by asking: Is there a disadvantaged population benefitting from manufacturing packaging? Are there energy offsets such as wind or solar power to help mitigate energy use for packaging production? Are there by-products being made with the packaging waste that benefits others? Are the materials locally available or sourced from a local enterprise that will benefit the community? Following SL resource practices, companies providing natural, renewable, biodegradable, or reusable (second use) packaging materials such as coconut husk, Forest Stewardship-certified bamboo, myco foam—a product made from natural fibers and mushrooms, postconsumer waste-corrugated cardboard, and gaemi wrap waffle cut paper—become important.

Some examples of successful SL resources in channels include Nooka, Inc. This New York-based company founded by designer Matthew Waldman creates lifestyle products focused on the intersection of design and technology (Nooka 2016). The design extends beyond its products to the packaging as well. Walderman points out, "about 80 million tons of waste is generated from packaging and containers annually according to the US environmental protection agency" (Nooka 2016). Nooka crowdsources innovative package design via its online Nooka Packaging competition using Adobe's Behance platform, seeking entries that have designs that are reusable or have a minimal environmental impact. Some examples of Nooka's success are a watch package which has a second use as a food bowl and an award-winning glue-less custom box that requires minimal material and labor, and is biodegradable.

Another example of SL resources in channels solution is the option to purchase product in bulk, using one's own containers. Dr. Bronner's liquid soap is an example of this. Bulk containers of soap equipped with pumps are available to customers at retail locations where they can bring their own containers to fill, eliminating the need for company-produced packaging altogether (Carpenter 2011). Besides conserving resources, benefitting others and having a lighter environmental footprint, sustainable packaging makes a great story for the company, further highlights one's commitment to sustainability, and can be developed as an important value proposition.

SL resources are also about delivery and emissions. Delivery options need just as careful consideration as packing especially in the area of energy use. In the United States, truck and rail transport account for nearly 60 % of freight transport in ton-miles and 80 % of the sector's greenhouse gas (GHG) emissions. GHG emissions from freight trucks increased by 80 % from 1980 to 2007, while the amount of freight shipped in trucks measured in ton-miles has grown by over 100 % in that same period. In 2009 alone, over 19 billion tons of freight, with a value of $13.3 trillion, was carried over 4.4 trillion ton-miles in the United States (EPA and DOT 2011). Creative solutions to minimize shipping costs, distances, and impacts include having local distribution or production facilities, consolidating deliveries, and using bicycles, horses, sailboats, or other nonfossil fuel delivery.

SL resources are also about waste. Many companies seek new customers via industry trade shows, which have a very heavy environmental footprint as display materials are shipped great distances, and waste is generated through flyers, disposable samples, and the impact of thousands of visitors. For example, the Outdoor Retailer trade show in Salt Lake City, Utah, has a Green Steps program where carpets are recycled, all waste recycled, and show materials are available electronically or minimally printed on recycled papers with soy inks. The result was that after 10,000 people visited a week-long trade show in Salt Lake City, Utah, almost 3 tons of cardboard and mixed recyclables were recycled (Outdoor Retailer 2010b).

SL health in relation to channels is about building relationships and stories through one's distribution. This includes working with an internal or contracted sales force to create memory, meaning, and identity. It is also a balance of work and play that values recreation and well-being. For example, New York-based Runa Tea, one of Inc Magazine's 500 Fastest Growing Companies, sends team members to Ecuador to visit the farming families they support (Runa 2016). Customers are also invited to participate in ecotourism projects Runa helps to develop in the area and participate in home stays and volunteer projects among the remote rainforest communities they work with (Runa 2016). These visits grow sustainability by enabling US staffers and customers to build new relationships and friendships with producers creating engaged learning experiences that strengthen the delivery and after sales experience for customer segments.

SL policy affects channels through base requirements companies can put on all distribution. For example, there can be a mandated radius where different delivery options become prioritized over others, such as bicycle courier delivery for all sales within a certain area, customer carpool pick-up options, bulk purchasing deals, or 100 % recycled or reusable packing. The challenge here is to make it communicated and representative—giving the customer a say in how this can happen.

SL exchange in channels supports creativity in how goods are accessed and strives for fair exchange, distribution, use, and welfare. This is where equality and local community support become important. To help goods become more accessible, local currencies can be accepted as a form of exchange along with volunteer time, trade, and local discounts. Products can be offered at different tiers with options of purchasing used goods or seconds being made available to lower income or more frugal members of the community. Excess product can also be donated to low-income distribution centers for a tax write off.

SL + channels = the most environmentally friendly ways of delivering and packaging goods.

Case Study—Artisan Beverage Cooperative

An example of how the SL is used with channels is seen in Massachusetts, US-based Artisan Beverage Cooperative (ABC). ABC wanted to expand distribution of their popular Katalyst Kombucha beverages. They were already bottling the product and had access to national distribution channels; however, they wanted something more sustainable and meaningful than mass production, excessive packaging through bottles, labels and cardboard carriers, and environmentally harmful cross-country shipping (Artisan Beverage Cooperative 2016). Being a cooperative, the team worked together to seek out different distribution options. It would have been easy to simply join existing distribution channels, work with established industry reps, and get into large grocery chains but they chose a more sustainable route instead. Deeply committed to minimizing their environmental footprint, creating opportunities for others, offering the freshest, most healthy product, and building community and mass shipping bottled goods to large retail outlets did not make sense. So instead they opted to set up a network of local Katalyst Kombucha breweries with keg, bulk, and locally bottled distribution. They still had a presence in large-chain retail outlets and produced some packaging, but they also had local bars and restaurants serving their product on tap and had refilling stations in key retail locations where customers could refill their own containers (Katalyst Kambucha 2016).

In this scenario, SL resources were carefully used with the diversification and localization of distribution: bottles, refill stations, and direct consumption in local regions. SL health was considered as local breweries created more jobs and built skills while cooperative ownership engaged people more in decision making and strategizing channels. The SL policy set a standard for quality—a fresher product could be served without the need for pasteurization that killed some of the healthy microbes that are such an important part of Katalyst Kombucha. This addressed the awareness and evaluation parts of channels too, creating a compelling story and high-quality product for customers. SL exchange was diversified through different levels of access, either through the discounted cost of bulk refills or the convenience of chain store distribution or the local camaraderie of sharing a brew in a local eatery. In addition, there are investment shares offered in the company creating another way that people can participate in the organization by supporting and gaining from its growth.

Customer Relationships

The customer relationships is the area most often overlooked in traditional marketing campaigns but the one that presents the most opportunities to attract new customers—otherwise known as acquisition and maintain long-term relationships—known in marketing terms as retention, grow sales through word of mouth—in marketing terminology: expansion, build community, and have a lot of fun. Social media makes this area especially interesting to engage in with so many new options being developed almost daily. There are different categories of customer relationships with businesses often embracing several at once. These include personal assistance which is a traditional customer–salesperson relationship either in person, on the phone or online; customized assistance where a dedicated service provider or contact specifically works with personal customers they have gotten to know over time; self-service where customers select the goods they want without any outside assistance or intervention; automated services where specially selected goods are suggested often based on online algorithms or publically available demographical data; communities or shared interest groups that are often intentionally formed by a business and enable the exchange information, shared problem solving, and advocacy; and cocreation that empowers customers to participate in the relationship by rating products, giving reviews and creating publically shared content (Osterwalder and Pigneur 2010).

Looking at customer relations with CL resources many new opportunities emerge to strengthen the customer relationship while also having a positive impact on the planet and community. One such way is to look at the product or service's entire life cycle and seeing how the business can continue to be a part of this, maintaining contact with the customer and helping them to engage in the full product life cycle. For example, there can be warranties, repair services, replacement parts, how-to videos, workshops, buy back, upcycling, and recycling associated with goods sold. As a company, one is taking full responsibility for their product and all if it impacts while also forming a stronger, long-term, collaborative relationship with the customers.

My company KUSIKUY offers many CL resources opportunities through several different practices. Our goal is for products to be used for many years and never enter into the waste stream. We offer single replacement gloves if just one I lost, that way the set can continue to be used. We also have a 5-year guarantee with free darning for knitwear plus a $20 buyback program which gives customer company credit to use on new purchases. Once we receive back product in the buyback program, it is unraveled and re-knit into blankets and sweaters for orphans in Bolivia (KUSIKUY 2016).

SL health illuminates more ways in which customer relationships can be built through love, inclusion, celebrations, and trust. As a company engages in the SL health, greater relationships and transparency is built, making it easier and more authentic to share with customers. Social media, smartphones, and other online platforms provide great opportunities for growing relationships within the organization and customer segments. Here profiles of producers, employees, and customers can be created and shared, messages sent back between workers, producers and the public, surveys, company trips, buyer recognition programs, newsletters and other online exchanges developed.

Looking at SL policy is about taking action and making the tools developed in SL health work, linking workers, producers, consumers more interactive and making them a regular part of the organizational operations. This can happen on a website, product packaging, through sales people signing people up for memberships, the creation of online communities and giving customers cocreation tools. This will very tightly link customers to the organization, give all a role and place in helping to guide decisions toward more sustainable outcomes, get people more involved and committed to organizational goals, and encourage them to share and include more people within the network. An example of the use of cocreation is seen in the online fashion retailer, Taylor Stitch, where consumers can visit the workshop to vote for their favorite designs by pre-buying handmade clothing (Taylor Stitch 2016).

SL exchange aspect of customer relationships is about creating ways for customers to continue to engage with one's company and product in a meaningful way. If an item is individually made there can be a link to the producer where a relationship is formed between the two or there can be a giving back or adoption element where customers are linked to opportunities to help others in the organization. An example of this is seen in KIVA nonprofit organization which allows people to lend money via the Internet to low-income entrepreneurs and students in over 80 countries

(KIVA 2016). Kiva's mission is "to connect people through lending to alleviate poverty" (KIVA 2016). This is done via loan profiles where investors can select who they want to fund and get continued updates on the status of the funding and use of the loan. Once the loans are repaid, investors can give these funds to someone else in the network (KIVA 2016). SL exchange is also about wealth, distribution, power, and advocacy. By educating customers, giving them tools, and empowering them to help with the distribution of resources, opportunities for customers to make the world a better place for all emerge. Making this shareable is also important for spreading the word and building community around meaningful change.

SL + customer relations = empowering others to get involved with products and people in a personal, meaningful way.

Note: The Sustainability Lens Culture Shift

As one engages in proactive, innovative, diverse ways at approaching sustainability from many angles, one's business develops a culture of innovation and change. Through example and personal decisions, sustainability is shared and built. Members within the business may begin to emerge as thought leaders and become known as doers, innovators, and creative problem solvers. The business itself may rise to become an important community leader, asset and an inspiration for others. Any organization and individual can use the SL, however, for a business, as it goes more deeply into exploring and pursuing SL opportunities, the culture may naturally shift to become more like one of a social enterprise.

CHAPTER 5

The Theoretical Impact of the Sustainability Lens

Abstract This chapter takes a step back to look at the sustainability lens and social entrepreneurship as sustainable development from the perspective of Amartya Sen's ideas of justice and the capabilities approach. In addition, it examines the types of enterprises and how each scales to different degrees of social responsibility.

Keywords Amartya Sen · Justice · Well-being · Happiness · Women · Social responsibility

As much as the sustainability lens (SL) can seem like a practical, how-to business tool, it can also be understood from a theoretical perspective. The following examines the theoretical impact of the SL from an interdisciplinary interpretation of economic theory.

Amartya Sen's Justice and Well-Being

Building social enterprises for sustainable development includes building justice: justice for the earth, people, and future generations. Justice in this sense can be understood as fairness, balance, and a place where all voices are heard with equal power and importance. However, there are

T.L. Stenn, *Social Entrepreneurship as Sustainable Development*,
DOI 10.1007/978-3-319-48060-2_5

two sides to justice: that which is realized and felt and that which is made up of rules, regulations, and consequences. Similar to Suma Qamana, justice cannot be isolated; injustices impact justice. For example, one cannot claim to have a free, fair justice system if certain populations are prosecuted more than others. The injustice of wrongful prosecution taints justice overall; just like someone's perfectly constructed sustainable town with local production, currencies, shared resources, and heartfelt celebrations are trumped by the town next door that is struggling and doing poorly.

Injustice is inequality meaning people and the planet are not being treated fairly, consistently, and in a meaningful way. There is vulnerability in inequality; the have-nots will want what the haves have and in time there will be confrontation. In this way, justice becomes a global concept and a key component of sustainable development.

To more deeply explore justice, one can turn to the work of Amartya Sen, a Nobel Laureate economist who is globally recognized for his work on justice. The English language does not allow a large enough vocabulary for the full examination of justice. Sen, who is of Indian descent, uses Sanskrit vocabulary to help distinguish two significantly different ways of defining justice which enables a greater conversation about social entrepreneurship (SE), sustainable development, and justice to be realized. Nyaya is Sanskrit for a "comprehensive concept of realized justice" (Sen 2009, p. 20). While niti is Sanskrit for a more concrete, tangible, and narrowly applied, justice often in the form of rules, laws, and "organizational propriety and behavioral correctness" (2009, p. 20). The niti concept of justice is familiar to the Western thinker and refers to norms, standards, and regulations. A niti view of justice from the SL focuses on guidelines, compliance, and certifications—an approach seen in many of the Fair Trade, B Corp, and organic certifying programs. However, it is within the complexities and expansiveness of nyaya where a larger, transformational understanding of justice lies. Looking at justice through the SL with nyaya means understanding peoples' lives and how trade mixes through them. It includes the lives of business owners and consumers, institutional directors, political leaders, and producers; everyone touched by trade. A nyaya view of justice in SE focuses on broad, interconnected, complex relationships.

The nyaya view of justice is often counterintuitive to Western thinkers who are used to being linear and precise in their understanding of things. Nevertheless, trade extends beyond Western sensibilities and engages people from other, much larger, ways of thinking. For example, the indigenous women of Fair Trade handicraft associations in Bolivia have long memories. They worship their ancestors and earth gods, quote old ways of knowing, and are cyclical in thinking and organizing. They struggle with the linear, niti demands that certification programs present. However, niti from the perspective of Western people who are more linear and short term in their thinking may seem like a comfort, a tool that brings order and consistency to chaos. Sen, whose work figures prominently in justice studies, is from India, a non-Western culture that—like the culture of the indigenous women—embraces a larger and longer way of thinking. He understands the struggle with niti. Being a Western-trained scholar, Sen provides a bridge between the precise, linear, Western way of knowing he learned, and the larger looser, non-Western ways with which he grew up. The ability to engage both ways of knowing is important when examining justice within SE as it spans the linear West and the larger non-West in its complex, global, relations.

Justice, as defined by economist Amartya Sen, is the ability to realize freedoms garnered by social entrepreneurs that can affect capabilities through the development of skills and efficiencies. Justice also affects opportunities by generating income and market access. The goals of SE as sustainable development can include poverty reduction, community strengthening, preservation of resources, and human empowerment. How this is realized and experienced varies greatly for reasons beyond niti procedures and nyaya values of a social enterprise. This is because gender, culture, age, class, religion, education, and ability directly affect the way in which one is able to experience justice.

The majority of social entrepreneurs are men; however, women social entrepreneurs are essential for a healthy entrepreneurial ecosystem and healthy economic growth. According to the US Census Bureau, while from 2007 to 2012 the number of women-owned firms grew 27 %, women ownership still made up only a third of all firms in the United States (Mesenbourg 2010). In 2015, the Kaufman Foundation found that women are lax to participate in business accelerators and networking opportunities because the culture is not often gender inclusive (Fetsch 2015). Nevertheless, worldwide, thousands of women work in SE, making up 75 % of the producer members of the USA Fair Trade Federation (FTF) and 60 % of the producer members of the European World Fair Trade Federation (WFTO) (FTF 2012; WFTO 2011). Many are handicraft producers working in home-based cottage industries and have the extra burden of unpaid domestic tasks such as cooking, cleaning, child care, and family activities. In Guatemala, for example, women spend three times the amount of time at these tasks than men (Arnould et al. 2011). This is similar to findings worldwide. Women also have less control over their daily lives. The United Nations reports that many women have no say in vital everyday decisions such as their own health care, household purchases, or visits to relatives (UNIFEM 2011).

In order for a social enterprise to build sustainable development issues such as gender culture, age, class, religion education, and ability need to be taken into account. Using the SL one can increase income and economic stability for producers, create access to local credit, value organic certification, and bring in new benefits from diversification, structural improvements, and supply chain control. Lives are improved through economic growth; however, economic growth is just one aspect of one's well-being. An individual's advantage or happiness is also important, and economic gains do not necessarily create happiness.

Sen writes that an individual's advantage is judged by the person's "capability to do things he or she has reason to value" (2009, p. 231). Happiness is understood as a feeling of self-satisfaction both personally and within one's community, which includes one's ability to achieve different combinations of functionings that can be compared and judged against each other in terms of what one had "reason to value" (Sen 2009). In order for social entrepreneurs to build sustainability, participants' functionings, as well as their economic advantage, need to be considered. For example, women producers in Bolivia identified six functions that were important to them and affected their well-being. These were education, family, social status, confidence, finances, and personal health and environmental health (Stenn 2013). Of these, only one had an economic focus. This is where the four parts of the SL become important. SL resources address the functionings of environmental health while SL health relates to functionings of social status, family, confidence, and personal health. SL policy is aligned with education where training and skills development can be a core value of the business. SL exchange addresses financial functionings.

Sometimes people do not even know what is needed for their well-being, especially if they are living in "survival mode" stressed by economic pressures, an unstable environment, and/or are deprived of opportunity. People do not have the luxury to imagine something better when they are trying to survive in their day-to-day lives. Deprived groups may be habituated to inequality, unaware of possibilities of social change, be hopeless about fulfillment, and be resigned to fate (Sen 2009). I worked with Bolivian women in Fair Trade for 13 years before the new constitution passed granting women legal rights and recognition. During this time, women were deprived of their basic rights; they had no legal access to land, had little education, and were considered possessions of their husbands. These women often sighed, threw up their arms, looked skyward, and declared that something would happen, "si Dios quiere" (if God wants it). They felt no power to make change themselves. Today these same women are educated, taking control of their communities, advocating for their needs and making sure their children graduate college. Sustainable development does not happen alone, social entrepreneurs can help, but culture and governance also have a direct effect in how it is experienced.

Sen's capability approach is about human freedom, and how it is assessed in terms of advantage and disadvantage. "In assessing our lives," wrote Sen, "we have reason to be interested not only in the kinds of lives we manage to lead but also in the freedom that we actually have to choose between different styles and ways of living" (2009, p. 227). As one achieves freedom through different combinations of functionings and grows their advantage, they experience greater justice. How this happens is as important as the fact that it happens; and whether what is achieved resulted from one's own agency or not is also significant. For example, receiving an expensive gift from a stranger can feel awkward, especially if one has nothing to offer in return. The inequality of the situation limits the amount of freedom one achieves from it. Having a nice gift to offer in return creates reciprocity and builds greater equality in the exchange, enabling both parties to feel better off. Sen further explains that one should be interested in "comprehensive outcomes," not just "culmination outcomes" putting the emphasis on how something works and not just what happens (2009, p. 251).

Using the capabilities approach entails looking at the kinds of lives people manage to lead, and the freedom they have to choose between different styles and ways of living. The capabilities approach is concerned with how one can achieve various combinations of functionings and compare and judge these against what one has to value (Sen 2009). This approach focuses on human life and not just "detached objects of convenience" such as income or possessions that so often are the criteria of human success (Sen 2009).

The substantially lens helps businesses to identify opportunities to build greater sustainability within the confines of the Business Model Canvas (BMC). The BMC is laid over the rough contours—mountains and valleys—of the cultural, political, and social landscape of the places where business happens. Being aware of the history, needs, and functionings of the people and environment is important when growing justice. How opportunities are understood and presented also affect how one experiences justice. This requires that a balance is sought between the niti rules of justice and the nyaya outcomes of the feeling of well-being.

The SL For-Profit and Nonprofit

Professor Thom Simmons has been studying the emergence of social enterprises with his students for 18 years and noticed certain benchmarks in how and where an organization develops a social mission. The following is a spectrum of social responsibility as seen in organizations spanning from for-profits to nonprofits. The result is the emergence of many hybrid models and innovative approaches for getting needs met. The SL is accessible and applicable to all organizations in this spectrum. Each has the power to grow sustainability by making well-informed, mindful choices that grow well-being for all (Table 5.1).

Table 5.1 Simmons (2016) scale of social responsibility

Level	*Legal structure*	*Characteristics*	*Examples*
I. Traditional and casual	For-profit	The lowest level of commitment to social responsibility. Firms are primarily concerned with profit, short-term cost reduction, and survival. Will frequently donate to causes when requested by local groups, but commitment is incidental, sporadic, and lacks long-term commitment.	Traditional Local Business Model
II. Self-defensive actor	For-profit	The company engages in social responsibility activities, but the motivation is specifically an effort to counter criticism of its products or policies. Precise marketing and public relations efforts attempt to polish a compromised brand image. Activity is reactionary.	Victoria's Secret: criticized for promoting negative female body image, responds by contributing to combat eating disorders and providing college scholarships to women.
III. Cyclical grantor	For-profit; often large public corporations	The company prefers to offer cash to other entities engaged in socially responsible work. Usually accomplished through creating a foundation, and offering cash grants on a cyclical basis. Little long-term commitment to a particular project, and minimal ongoing interaction with grant recipients.	Harley-Davidson: The Milwaukee-based motorcycle manufacturer establishes wide-ranging grant programs in communities where dealerships are located, in the area of education, environment, health care, and veterans' issues.

(*continued*)

Table 5.1 (continued)

Level	*Legal structure*	*Characteristics*	*Examples*
IV. Project focused	For-profit	This level represents a significant change in focus. The company has embraced, and is dedicated to, a particular cause or project and commits resources toward its long-term success.	Squeaky Wheel: A New-York based marketing firm, Squeaky Wheel has three dedicated employees who operate the IHadCancer.com website, a social media site dedicated to making connections between those affected by cancer. The website produces no income and is free to users, entirely subsidized by the company.
V. Operations focused	For-profit; many are closed corporations or employee owned	These companies focus their socially responsible approach on all aspects of their company's production and operations. Social responsibility is seen as internal to the company's existence, rather than as an external focus.	New Belgium Brewing (NBB): A Colorado craft brewer owned by its employees. NBB trains its employees in financial literacy to help make company financial decisions, utilizes renewable energy resources, promotes bicycle use over autos, and is committed to constant reductions in water and energy use.
VI. Social business venture	For-profit company; often closed corporation	The social business venture is legally organized as a for-profit company, but its mission is to fulfill a traditionally nonprofit purpose. Company profit is used to fulfill the mission.	Albergo Etico: An Italian hotel/restaurant, whose purpose is to educate and train people with Down syndrome for independent living. Hotel and restaurant profits support the living, education, and training expenses of the students. Tom's Shoes: A California-based closed corporation that sells shoes at a premium, allowing them to cover the cost of a second pair of shoes which is then donated to those in poverty in the United States and the developing world.

VII. Hybrid nonprofit	Nonprofit 501 (c) 3	The hybrid nonprofit is organized as a nonprofit corporation under the Internal Revenue Code for one of the purposes listed in IRS Regulation 501(c)3. However, rather than relying exclusively on traditional donations or fundraisers, the hybrid establishes for-profit businesses, all of whose profit is funneled back into the nonprofit to sustain funding and operations.	Housing Works: A New York City-based nonprofit, Housing Works provides housing, medical assistance, and other services to homeless and HIV-positive youth. Funding is raised, in part, through for-profit retail businesses including café-bookstores, furniture thrift shops, and T-shirt printing operations.
VIII. Pure nonprofit	Nonprofit 501 (c) 3	As in Level VII, the pure nonprofit is organized as a Non-Profit Corporation under the Internal Revenue Code for one of the purposes listed in IRS Regulation 501(c)3. However, the organization shies away from profitable business ventures to fund itself; rather, it relies on traditional means of financial support, such as fundraising events, donations, and awareness campaigns. Some may charge fees for services or memberships.	American Heart Association; Humane Society; YMCA.

References

ABC. (2016). Artisan Beverage Cooperative. Retrieved September 8, 2016 from http://artbev.coop/.

Aguilar, R. G. & Skar, S. A. (2014). *Rhythms of the Pachakuti: Indigenous Uprising and State Power in Bolivia*. Duke University Press Books.

Alexosterwalder. (2016). Hi! I'm Alex Osterwalder. Retrieved August 31, 2016 from http://alexosterwalder.com/.

Arnould, E., Plastina, A. & Ball, D. (September 2011). Alternative Trade Organization and subjective quality of life: The case of Latin American coffee producers. *Journal of Macromarketing*, *31*(3): 276–290.

Artaraz, K., & Calestani, M. (20 August 2014). Suma Qamana in Bolivia: Indigenous understandings of well-being and their contribution to a post-neoliberal paradigm in Bolivia. Latin American Perspectives. Sage Publications.

Baer, D. (28 February 2014). How Patagonia's new CEO is increasing profits while trying to save the world. Fast Company. Retrieved August 27, 2016 from http://www.fastcompany.com/3026713/lessons-learned/how-patagonias-new-ceo-is-increasing-profits-while-trying-to-save-the-world.

Battiste, M. (2002). Indigenous knowledge and pedagogy in first nations education a literature review with recommendations. Minister of Indian and Northern Affairs, INAC. Canada.

B Corp. (2016). What are B Corps? Retrieved August 29, 2016 from https://www.bcorporation.net/.

BerkShares. (2016). Using BerkShares - how it works. Retrieved August 31, 2016 from http://www.berkshares.org/how_to_spend.

Blackman, A., & Rivera, J. (2010). Producer-level benefits of sustainability certification. *Conservation Biology*, *25*(6): 1176–1185.

T.L. Stenn, *Social Entrepreneurship as Sustainable Development*,
DOI 10.1007/978-3-319-48060-2

Borden, L. (1 October 2014). How my family celebrates a healthier Halloween. Huffington Post. Retrieved September 6, 2016 from http://www.huffingtonpost.ca/lisa-borden/reverse-trick-or-treating_b_5868966.html.
Bradley, L. (2010). The butterfly effect. Chaos and Fractals. Space Telescope Science Institute. Baltimore, MD.
Bump, P. (21 April 2015). The very simple reason more money is spent on lobbyists than on Congress. The Washington Post, DC.
Businessmodelalchemist. (2016). Business model alchemist. Retrieved August 31, 2016 from http://businessmodelalchemist.com/.
Businessmodelgeneration. (2016). Business model generation. Retrieved August 31, 2016 from http://www.businessmodelgeneration.com/book.
Carpenter, S. (October 2011). Buy in bulk: Those big bins mean fewer recyclables. L.A. at Home. LA Times. October 14, 2011.
CDC. (2015). National Institute for Occupational Safety and Health (NIOSH) Education and Information Division. Retrieved Nov. 6, 2016 from: http://www.cdc.gov/niosh/ershdb/emergencyresponsecard_29750038.html.
Chandler, R. (2005). Strategic planning for organizational "integrity" continuity is essential for avoiding, mitigating, and surviving organizational scandals and (un)ethical disasters. *Graziadio Business Review, 8*(3). https://gbr.pepperdine.edu/2010/08/avoiding-ethical-misconduct-disasters/.
Choquehuanca, D. (2010). *Vivir Bien. Ministery of Foreign Relations.* Bolivia: International Institute of Integration, III-CAB.
circlesofsustainability.org. (2014). About our Approach. Retrieved November 6, 2016.
Creativecommons. (2016). What we do. Retrieved August 31, 2016 from https://creativecommons.org/about/.
Crutchfield, L., & McLeod Grant, H. (2012). *Forces for good.* CA: Jossey-Bass.
Dabla-Norris, E., Kochhar, K., Ricka, F., Suphaphiphat, N., & Tsounta, E. (June 2015). Causes and consequences of income inequality: A global perspective. International Monetary Fund: Strategy, Policy, and Review Department.
Dees, G. (October 1998). *The Meaning of Social Entrepreneurship.* Kansas City, MO and Palo Alto, CA: Kauffman Foundation and Stanford University.
Duhigg, C., & Barboza, D. (25 January 2012). In China, human costs are built into an iPad. New York Times.
Dunne, D. & Martin, R. (2006). Design Thinking and How It Will Change Management Education: An Interview and Discussion. *Academy of Management Learning & Education*, *5*(4), 512–523.
Ellis, B. (2012). Funny money? 11 local currencies. CNN Money. Retrieved August 31, 2016 from http://money.cnn.com/galleries/2012/pf/1201/gallery.community-currencies/.
EPA & DOT. (August 2011). Final rulemaking to establish greenhouse gas emissions standards and fuel efficiency standards for medium- and heavy-duty engines and vehicles. Regulatory impact analysis. Report no. EPA-420-R-11-901.

Equal Exchange. (2016). About. Retrieved August 28, 2016 from http://equal exchange.coop/about.
ERM. (2013). Five basics to managing innovation risk. Enterprise Risk Management Initiative (ERM), Poole College of Management. North Carolina State University.
Everlane.com. (2016). Radical transparency. Retrieved August 28, 2016 from https://www.everlane.com/about.
Fair Trade Federation. (2012). About us. Retrieved November 11, 2012 from http://fairtradefederation.org/ht/d/sp/i/177/pid/177.
Fetsch, E. (16 February 2015). Why the lack of women leaders is a problem for businesses. Growthology. The Kauffman Foundation. Retrieved September 9, 2016 from http://www.kauffman.org/blogs/growthology/2015/02/why-the-lack-of-women-leaders-is-a-problem-for-businesses.
FINE. (2006). *Business unusual*. Brussels: Fair Trade Advocacy Office.
Forcesforgood. (2016). Our findings. Retrieved September 2, 2016 from http://www.forcesforgood.net/findings.html.
FSC. (2016). Our history. FSC United States. Retrieved August 30, 2016 from https://us.fsc.org/en-us/who-we-are/our-history.
Fuji Xerox. (August 2013). Fuji Xerox Australia sustainability report 2013. Fuji Xerox Australia Pty Limited. Australia.
Garcia, J., Lozano, A., Olivera, J., & Ruiz, C. (2004). *Learning wisdom and the good way to live*. Ecuador: Amawtay Wasi Cross Cultural University. Imprenta Mariscal.
Global Exchange. (2016). Get your reverse trick or treating kit today. Retrieved September 6, 2016 from http://www.globalexchange.org/get-your-reverse-trick-or-treating-kit-today.
Goldstein, D. (Spring 1998). Performing national culture in a Bolivian migrant community. *Ethnology*, *37*(2): 117–132. Special Issue: Relocating Bolivia: Popular Political.
Gupta, A. (2003). *Postcolonial developments*. Durham: Duke University Press.
Haney, B. (2007). The price of sugar. Uncommon Productions.
Harper, D. (November 2001). Online etymology dictionary. Retrieved October 27, 2007.
Hernandez Navarro, L. (12 March 2012). Bolivia has transformed itself by ignoring the Washington Consensus. The Guardian. Retrieved August 27, 2016 from https://www.theguardian.com/commentisfree/cifamerica/2012/mar/21/bolivia-washington-consensus.
Hartwick. (2012). Harlow farm is "sharing the harvest". Retrieved November 6, 2016 from: http://www.hardwickagriculture.org/blog/harlow-farm-is-sharing-the-harvest.
Holmgren, D. (2002). *Permaculture: Principles & pathways beyond sustainability*. Canada: Holmgren Design Services. New Society Publishers.
Hopkins, R. (2008). *The transition handbook*. Vermont: Chelsea Green Publishing.

Hopkins, R. (2011). *The transition companion.* Vermont: Chelsea Green Publishing.
Huanacuni Mamani, F. (2010). *Vivir Bien/Buen Vivir, 4th edition. Coordinadora Andina de Organizaciones Indigenas, CAOI.* Peru: Lima.
IMS Barter. (2016). About IMS barter. Retrieved August 28, 2016 from: https://www.imsbarter.com/about-ims-barter.
James, P. (2015). *Urban Sustainability and Theory in Practice.* Earthscan from Routledge.
Katalyst Kambucha. (2016). Tap program. Retrieved September 8, 2016 from http://katalystkombucha.com/tap-program/.
Kawano, E., Masterson, T., & Teller-Elsberg, J. (2009). *Social solidarity economy: Building alternatives for people and planet. Center for popular economics.* Amherst: UMass.
Kennedy, J. (27 September 1960). Remarks of Senator John F. Kennedy, Municipal Auditorium, Canton, Ohio. The American Presidency Project. University of California.
Kiva.org (2016). About Us. Retrieved November 6, 2016 from: https://www.kiva.org/about.
KUSIKUY.com (2016). Extreme Suretrievedty. Retrieved November 6, 12016 from: http://www.kusikuy.com/terms-of-service/.
Lentil as Anything. (2016). About. Retrieved September 8, 2016 from http://lentilasanything.com/about/.
Lozada, C. (April 1991). Overgrazing and range degradation in the Peruvian Andes. *Rangelands, 13*(2): 64–67. Elsevier. P.
Mesenbourg, T. (7 December 2010). Women-owned businesses. Random Samplings. US Census Bureau.
Miller, E. (2013). Community economy: Ontology, ethics, and politics for radically democratic economic organizing. *Rethinking Marxism, 25*(4): 518–533.
Monni, S., & Pallottino, M. (2013). Beyond growth and development: Buen Vivir as an alternative to current paradigms. Working Paper n°172. Dipartimento di EconomiaUniversità. Università degli Studi Roma Tre. Italy.
NCA. (2014). NCA's 2014 Annual Confectionery Industry review. Retrieved September 6, 2016 from http://www.candyusa.com/data-insights/state-of-the-confectionery-industry/.
New Belgium. (2016). Values and stories. Retrieved September 6, 2016 from http://www.newbelgium.com/sustainability.
Noguchi, Y. (28 August 2015). Comparing the top boss's pay to yours. All things considered. National Public Radio, NPR.
Nooka. (2016). About. Nooka, Inc. Retrieved August 2, 2016 from www.nooka.com/.
OCA. (2016). Genetic Engineering – what you need to know. Retrieved November 6, 2016 from: https://www.organicconsumers.org/categories/genetic-engineering.

O'Keefe, B. (March 2016). Bitter sweets. Fortune magazine.

Osterwalder, A. (2004). The business model ontology - A proposition in a design science approach. PhD thesis, University of Lausanne. France.

Osterwalder, A., & Pigneur, Y. (2010). *Business model generation*. New York: Wiley Publishing.

OTA. (2016). Advocacy. Retrieved November 6, 2014 from: https://www.ota.com/advocacy.

Outdoor Retailer. (2010). Sustainability. Retrieved September 8, 2016 from http://www.outdoorretailer.com/sustainability.shtml, 2010.

RIPESS. (2016). About us. Intercontinental network for the promotion of social solidarity economy, RIPESS. Retrieved August 30, 2016 from http://www.ripess.org/about-us/?lang=en.

Ries, E. (2011). *The Lean Startup*. Crown Business.

Runa. (2016). Impact. Retrieved August 30, 2016 from runa.org/impact/#social-impact.

Sanchez, L. (2013). Thinking and doing the ethic of liberation and Buen Vivir in 21st century Ecuador. Andean Cosmologies in the Ontological Crisis of the 21st Century. State University of New York, Albany.

Sarango, L. (2009). *La Universidad Intercultural de las Nacionalidades y Pueblos Indígenas "Amawtay Wasi."* Caracas: Instituto Internacional de la UNESCO para la Educación Superior en América Latina y el Caribe (UNESCO-IESALC). 191–214. Quito, Ecuador: Mariscal Publishers.

Schlossberg, M. (18 October 2015). No one pays full price anymore—And it's terrifying companies. Business Insider. Businessinsider.com.

Segran, E. (July 2016). How sundial brands CEO richelieu dennis is challenging segregation in the beauty aisle. Fast Company magazine.

Semco.com. (2016). Joint-venture catalysts for expansion in Brazil. Retrieved August 28, 2016 from http://www.semco.com.br/en/.

Semler, R. (2004). *The seven-day weekend*. New York: Penguin Group.

Sen, A. (2009). *The idea of justice*. Harvard: Balknap Press.

Simmons, T. (2016). *Simmons scale of social responsibility*. MA: Greenfield Community College.

Skoll Foundation. (2015). COP21: What Does Climate Deal Mean for Social Entrepreneurs? Retrieved November 6, 2016 from: http://skoll.org/2015/12/14/cop21-what-does-it-mean-for-social-entrepreneurs/.

Spies, G. J., Rhyne, R. H. Jr., Evans, R., Wetzel, K. E., Ragland, D. T., Turney, H. G., Leet, T. L., & Oglesby, J. L. (1995). Monitoring acrylic fiber workers for liver toxicity and exposure to dimethylacetamide. II: Serum clinical chemistry results of dimethylacetamide exposed workers. *Journal of Occupational Environmental Medicine*, 37(9): 1102–1107.

Stenn, T. (2013). *The cultural and political intersection of fair trade and justice*. NY: Palgrave Macmillan.

Stenn, T. (2015). Unlocking the secrets of Quinoa, a comparative study of Andean women quinoa producers. Human Development Capabilities Approach, HDCA conference paper. Georgetown University.

Stitch, T. (2016). Workshop. Retrieved September 8, 2016 from https://www.taylorstitch.com/collections/workshop.

Strategyzer.com. (2016). The business model canvas. Retrieved August 31, 2016 from https://strategyzer.com.

SundialBrands. (2016). About us. Retrieved September 6, 2016 from http://www.sundialbrands.com/about-us/.

Taub, S. (19 June 2002). Crisis of ethics: Ethics officers predict a new wave of corporate scandals. CFO.COM. Retrieved August 27, 2016 from http://www.cfo.com/article.cfm/3005220?f=search.

Thompson, L. (Fall 2010). Climate change: The evidence and our options. *Behaviour Analyst*, *33*(2): 153–170.

Thomson, B. (2011). Pachakuti: Indigenous perspectives, buen vivir, sumaq kawsay and degrowth. *Development*, *54*(4): 448–454.

Tulane University. (July 2015). Final report: 2013/14 survey research on child labor in West African cocoa growing areas. School of Public Health and Tropical Medicine, Tulane University.

UNIFEM. (2011). *Gender justice: Key to achieving the millennium development goals*. NY: UNIFEM.

Vecsey, C., & Venables, R. W. (1994). *American Indian environments: Ecological issues in Native American history*. New York: Syracuse University Press.

Villenueve-Smith, F., & Temple, N. (2015). State of social enterprise report. Social Enterprise, UK.

Webber, J. (2011). *From rebellion to reform in Bolivia*. Chicago, IL: Haymarket Books.

Woll, L. (16 March 2015). Voices: Lisa Woll, on the rise of social-impact investing. Markets. *The Wall Street Journal*. Retrieved November 2, 2016 from: http://www.wsj.com/articles/voices-lisa-woll-on-the-rise-of-social-impactinvesting-1426519119.

World Fair Trade Organization. (6 October 2011). 10 principles of fair trade. Retrieved August 30, 2012 from http://www.wfto.com/index.php?option=com_content&task=view&id=2&Itemid=14.ion=com_content&task=view&id=2&Itemid=14.

Worrall, A. (February 2015). Lean takings as tightwad diners exploit lentil as anything's philosophy. GoodFood.com. Retrieved September 8, 2016 from http://www.goodfood.com.au/eat-out/news/lean-takings-as-tightwad-diners-exploit-lentil-as-anythings-philosophy-20150208-138wvk.

Yee, V. (14 March 2016). Tainted-water worries spread to Vermont Village. New York Times. New York.

ZERI. (2016). Stone paper. Zero Emissions Research and Initiatives, ZERI. Retrieved August 31, 2016 from http://www.zeri.org/stone-paper.html.

Index

T.L. Stenn, *Social Entrepreneurship as Sustainable Development*,
DOI 10.1007/978-3-319-48060-2

The manufacturer's authorised representative in the EU is Springer Nature Customer Service Centre GmbH, Europaplatz 3, 69115 Heidelberg, Germany. If you have any concerns regarding our products, please contact ProductSafety@springernature.com

Printed and bound by CPI Group (UK) Ltd, Croydon, CR0 4YY
30/09/2026
02225609-0004